THIS BOOK BELONGS TO:

_____

....

_____

_____

....

_____

HOW TO DRAW
ADORABLE AND EASY
500 DRAWINGS
OF ANIMALS, CARS, FOOD, GIFTS AND CUTE STUFF FOR KIDS

ISBN: 979-8-990881426
Copyright 2024 ©
Authored by Helen Booker

HOW TO USE THIS BOOK

The drawings in the book are in no prarticular order, so you can start from whereever you want. Just pick up simpler shapes to begin with, so you can get the hang of it.

Prepare your reliable and preferably soft pencil and eraser duo for a seamless drawing session. Opt for colored pencils to add vibrant hues into your masterpiece.

When drawing with your pencils, use delicate strokes for a tidy outline and effortless error correction. Press lightly, following the arrows to complete your artwork. Since there is no room to practice in the book, grab a some paper and start your drawing journey. Enjoy!

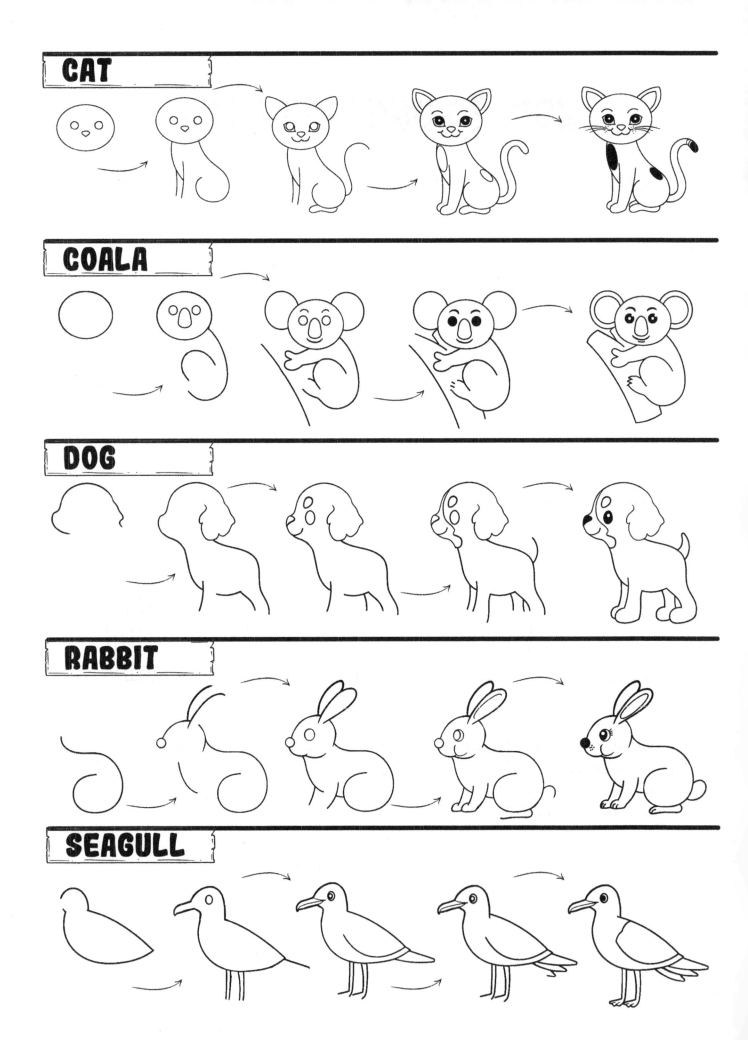

CAT

COALA

DOG

RABBIT

SEAGULL

PENGUIN

DOLPHIN

SQUID

CHAMELEON

STARFISH

BEAVER

SWORDFISH

SNAIL

CROCODILE

FROG

OCTOPUS

TURTLE

SEAHORSE

CRAB

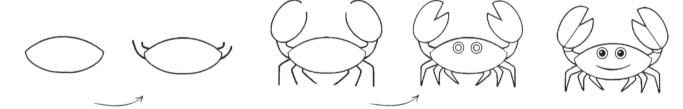

LADYBAG

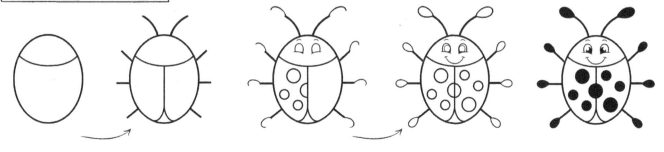

SEAL

HUMMINGBIRD

BUTTERFLY

SHARK

SNAKE

WHALE

OWL

SEASHELL

BAT

MOUSE

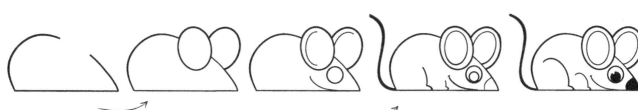

CAMEL

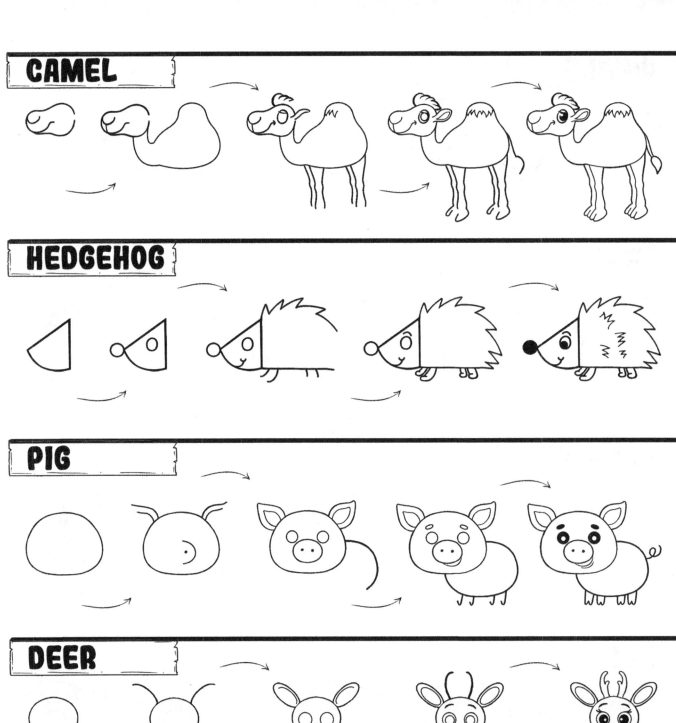

HEDGEHOG

PIG

DEER

DRAGONFLY

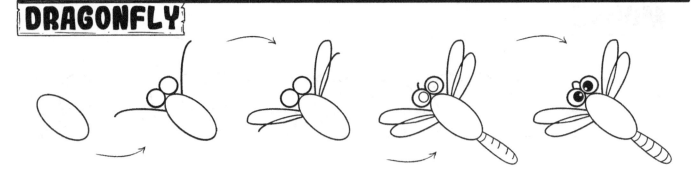

BEE

GIRAFFE

WORM

GOAT

DUCK

LLAMA

COW

CHICKEN

RACOON

NARWHAL

HORSE

LION

BEAR

WALRUS

MANTA RAY

FOX

PELICAN

LOBSTER

SHEEP

ZEBRA

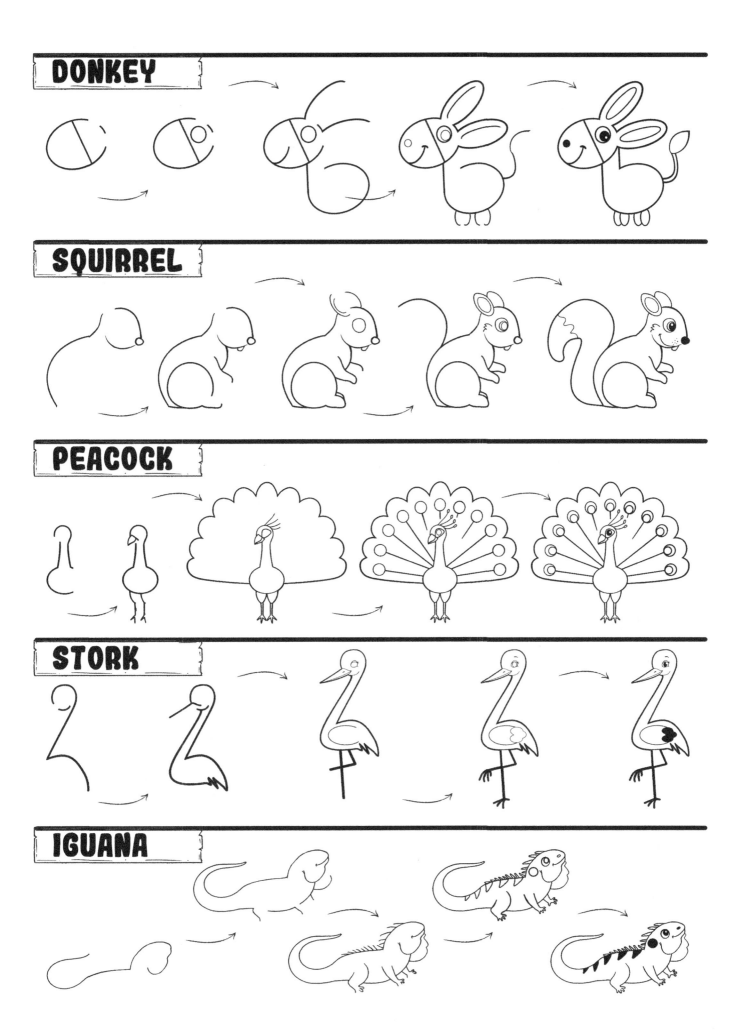

DONKEY

SQUIRREL

PEACOCK

STORK

IGUANA

CATERPILLAR

ELEPHANT

ANTEATER

EAGLE

ANT

TOUCAN

OSTRICH

HYENA

RHINOCEROS

SPIDER

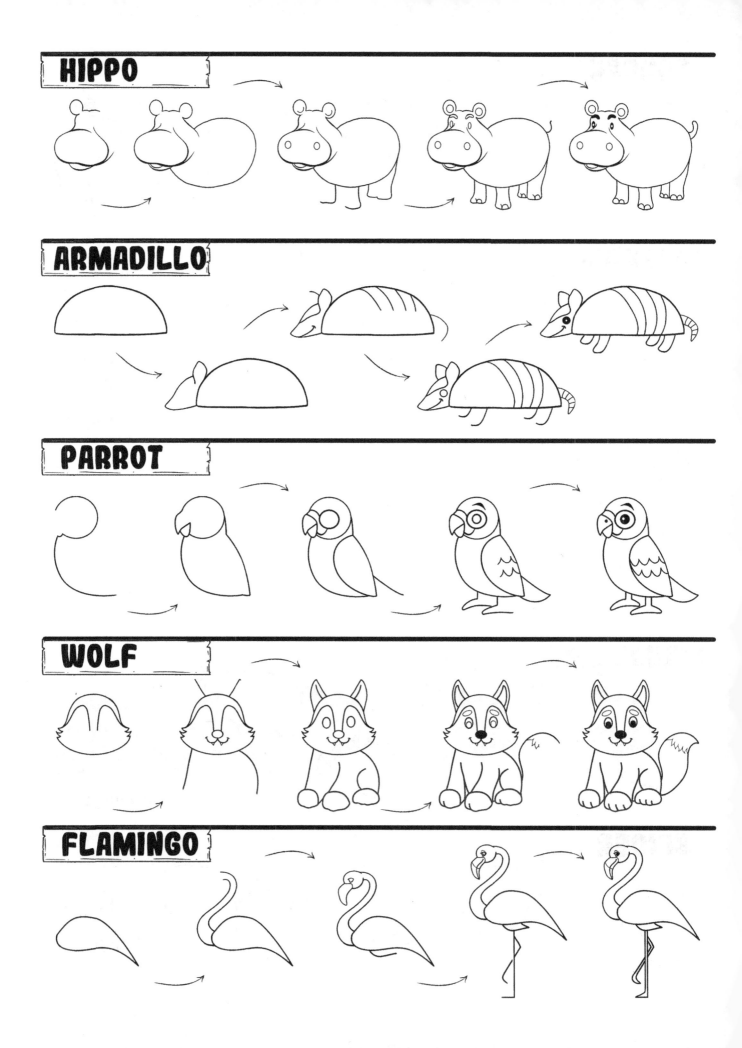

HIPPO

ARMADILLO

PARROT

WOLF

FLAMINGO

MONKEY

WILD BOAR

MOOSE

JELLYFISH

CRICKET

BULL

KANGAROO

SCORPION

TAPIR

TURKEY

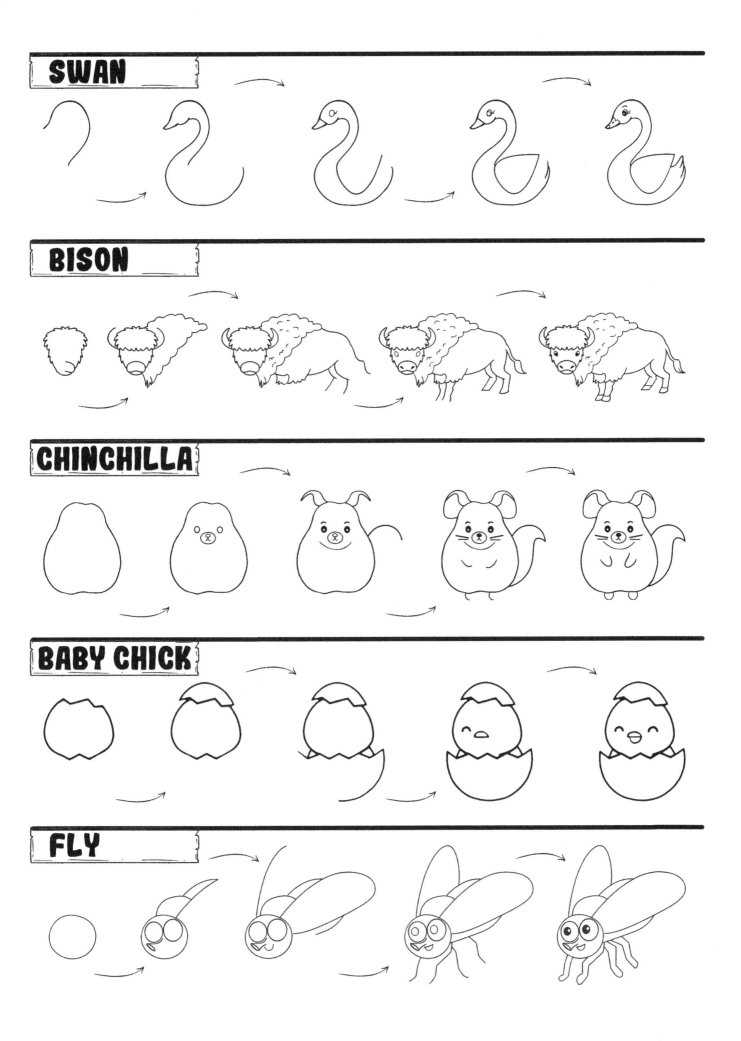

SWAN

BISON

CHINCHILLA

BABY CHICK

FLY

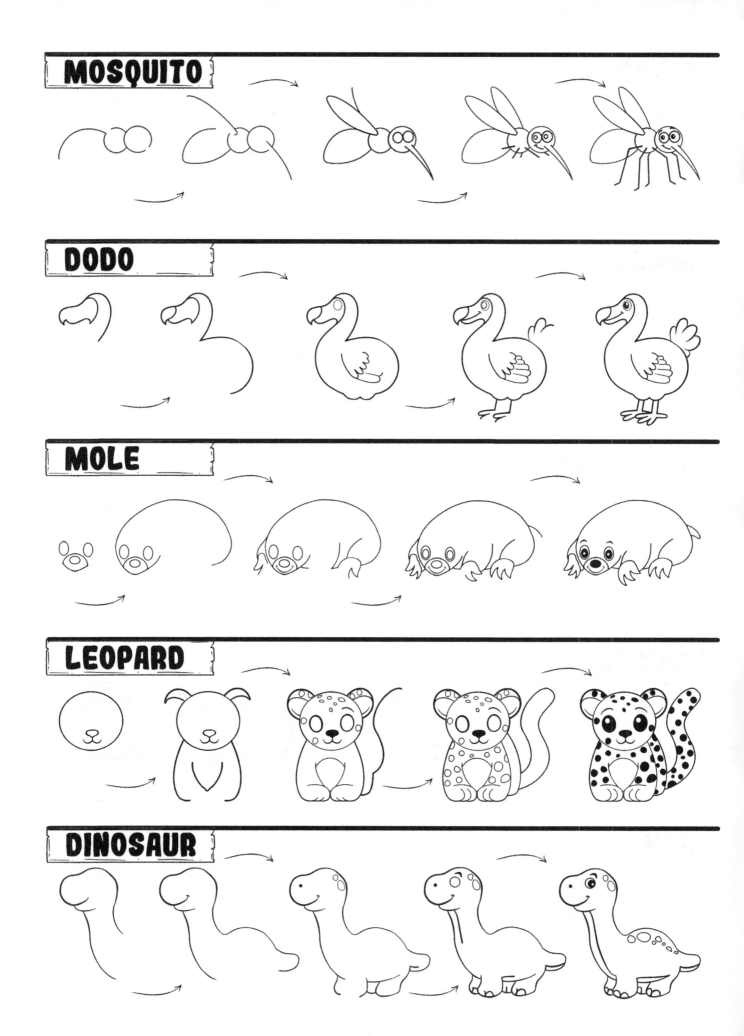

MOSQUITO

DODO

MOLE

LEOPARD

DINOSAUR

PORCUPINE

MEERKAT

SKUNK

DRAGON

LEMUR

KIWI

PIGEON

PTERODACTYL

POSSUM

TIGER

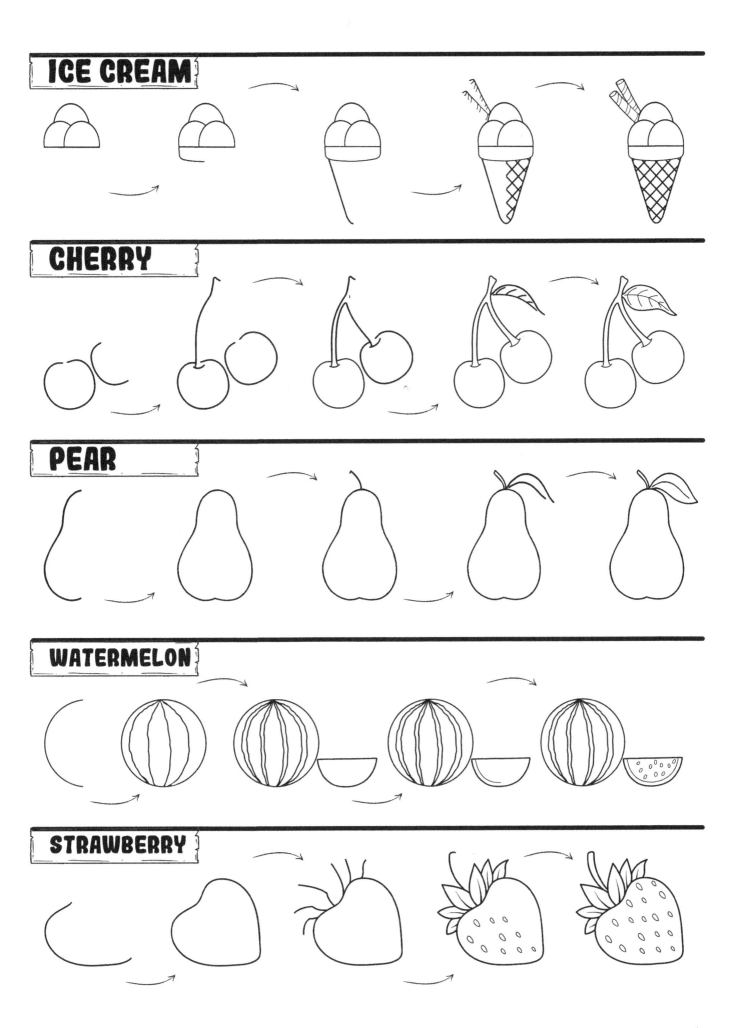

ICE CREAM

CHERRY

PEAR

WATERMELON

STRAWBERRY

APRICOT

BANANA

LEMON

APPLE

BLUEBERRY

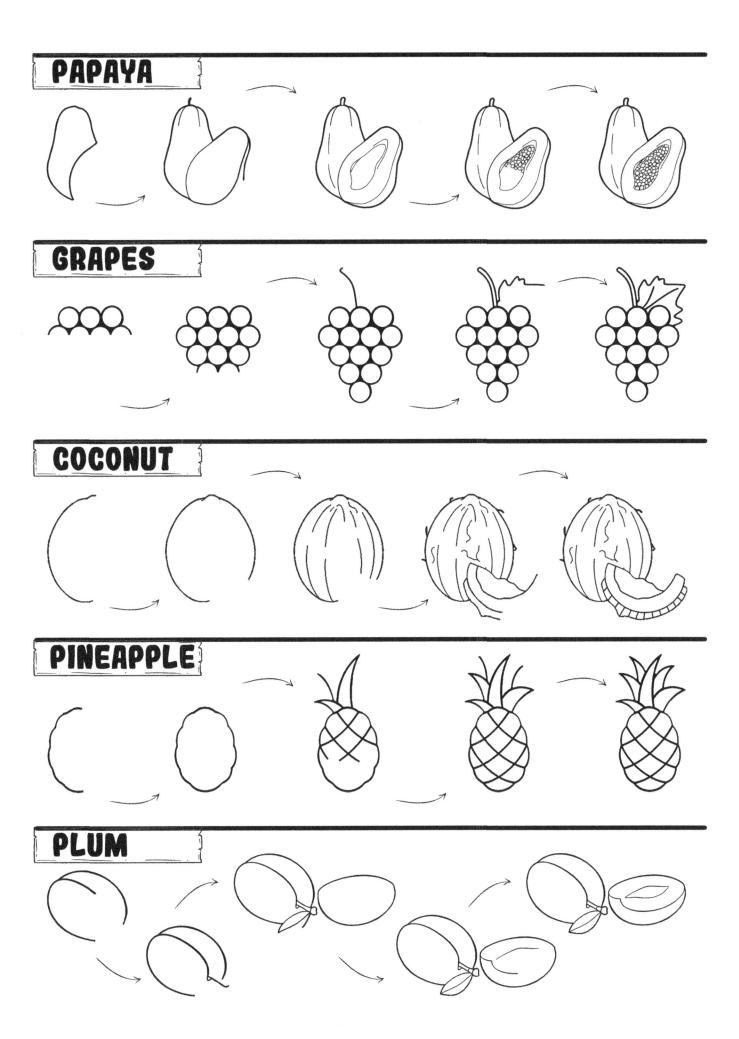

PAPAYA

GRAPES

COCONUT

PINEAPPLE

PLUM

ORANGE

FIG

BLACKBERRY

ASPARAGUS

EGGPLANT

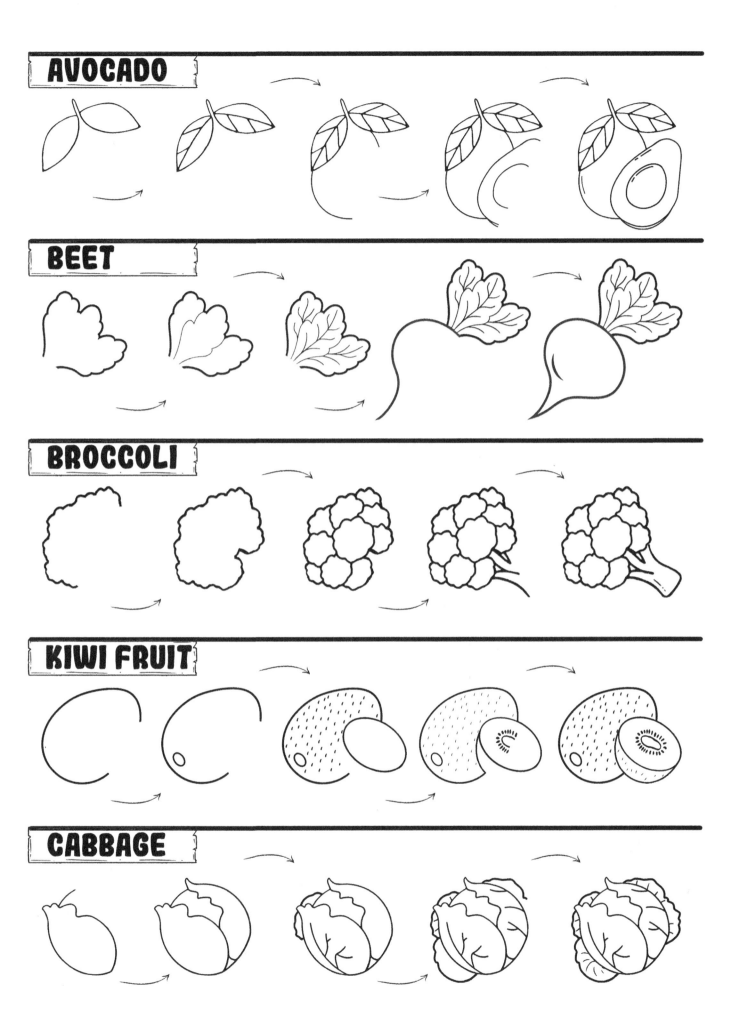

AVOCADO

BEET

BROCCOLI

KIWI FRUIT

CABBAGE

POMEGRANATE

CARROT

CAULIFLOWER

CELERY

CORN

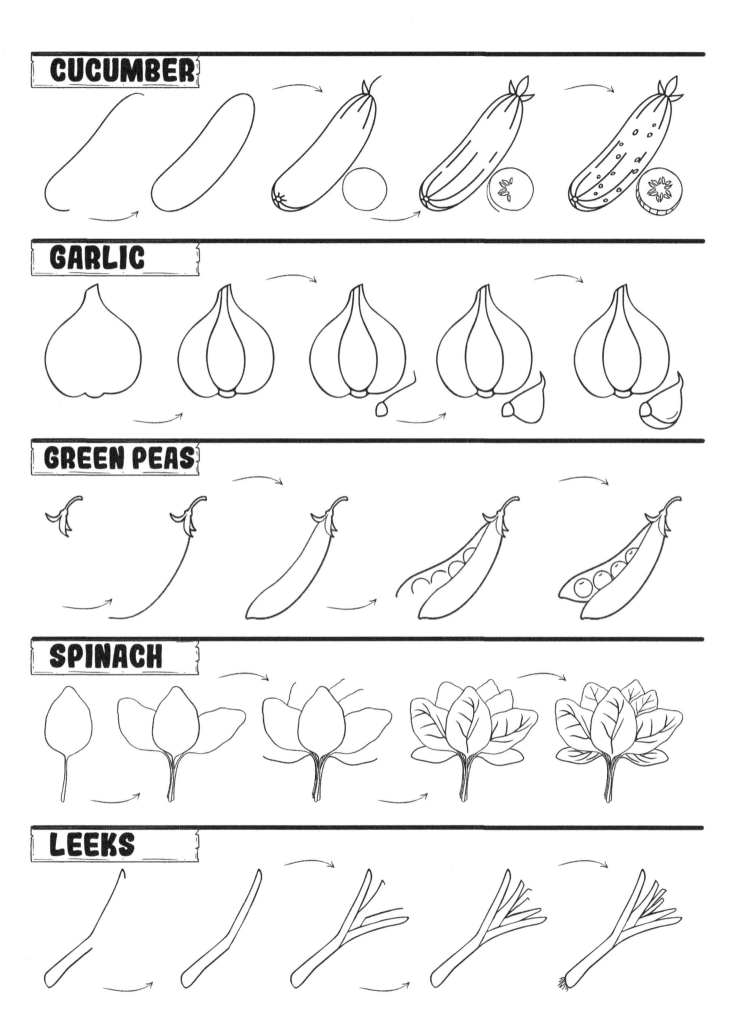

CUCUMBER

GARLIC

GREEN PEAS

SPINACH

LEEKS

LETTUCE

MUSHROOM

OKRA

PUMPKIN

CHILLI PEPPERS

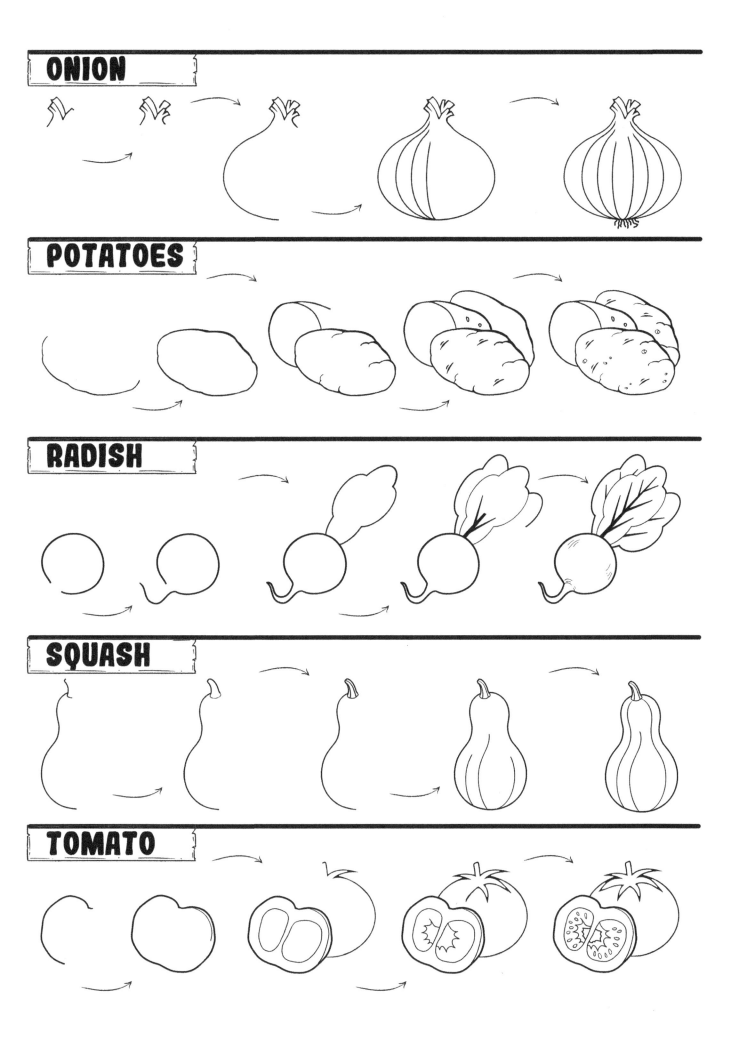

ONION

POTATOES

RADISH

SQUASH

TOMATO

CHESTNUTS

PRETZEL

HOT DOG

BEANS

ACORN

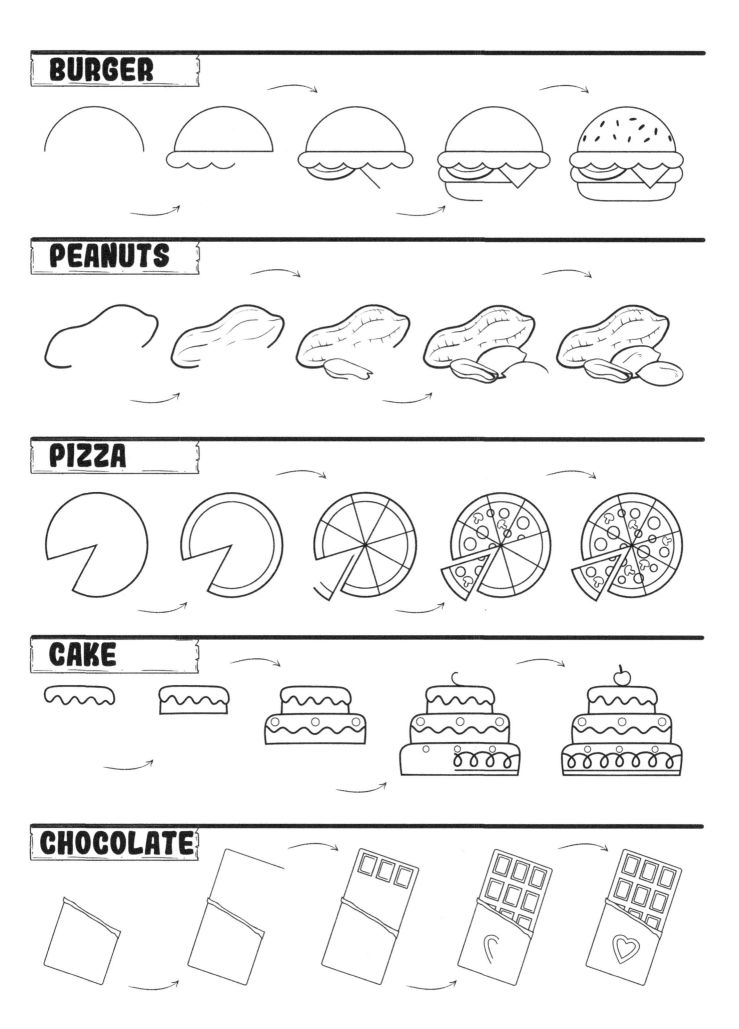

BURGER

PEANUTS

PIZZA

CAKE

CHOCOLATE

POPCORN

WAFFLE

JUICE

DONUT

COOKIES

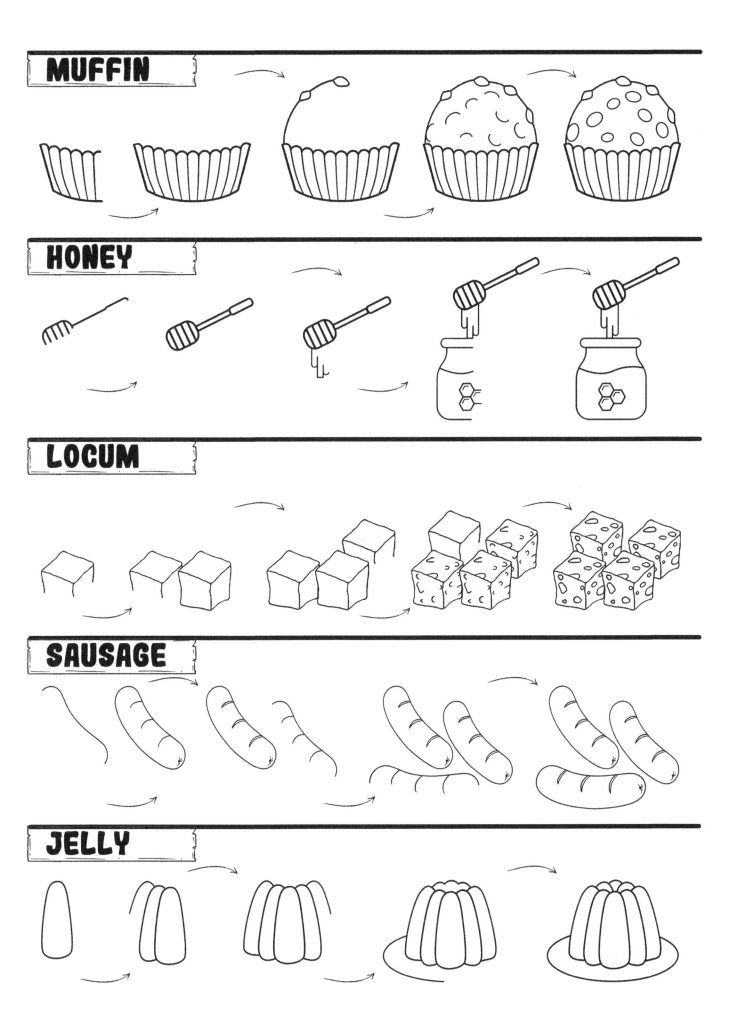

MUFFIN

HONEY

LOCUM

SAUSAGE

JELLY

PANCAKES

TEA

SOUP

CHIPS

BUTTER

BURRITO

MEATBALLS

FRENCH FRIES

CRACKERS

GRANOLA BAR

LOLLIPOP

TULUMBA

GINGERBREAD MEN

APPLE PIE

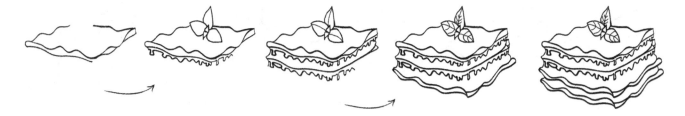

LASAGNA

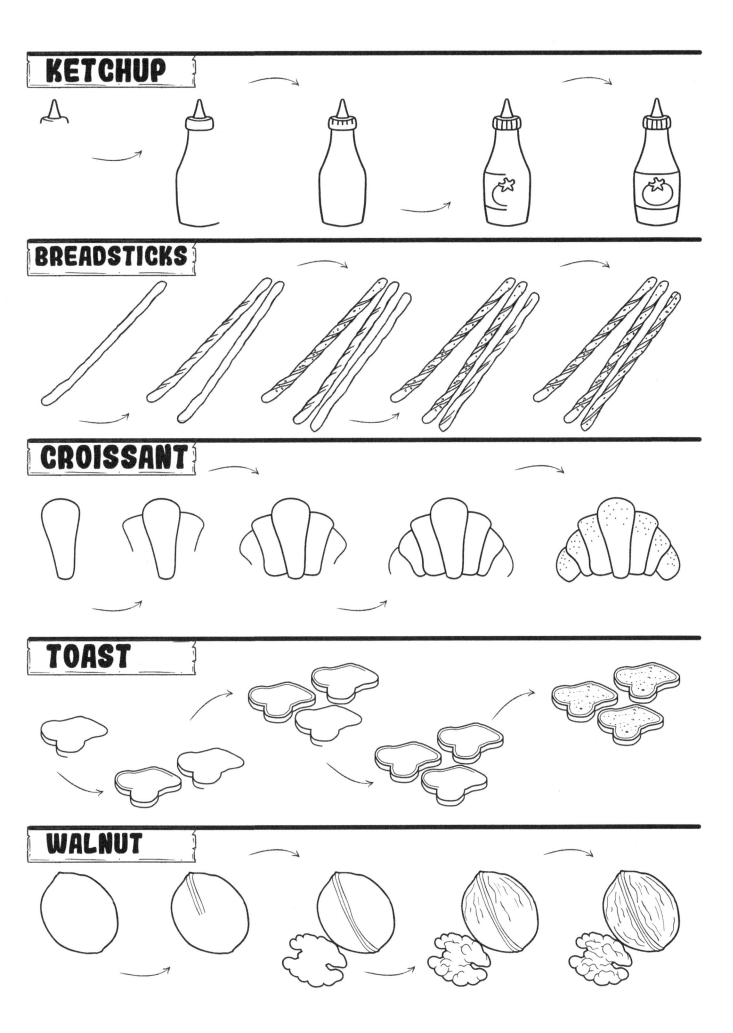

KETCHUP

BREADSTICKS

CROISSANT

TOAST

WALNUT

FRENCH BAGUETTE

ALMOND

WHEAT

FLATBREAD

SALT

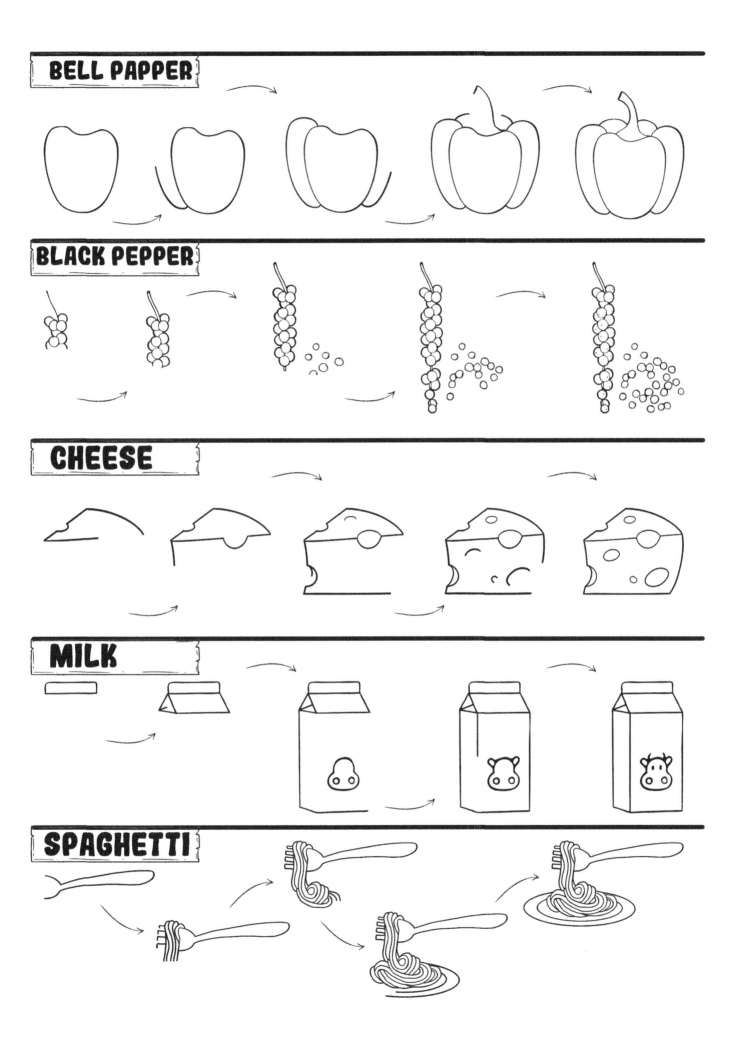

BELL PAPPER

BLACK PEPPER

CHEESE

MILK

SPAGHETTI

TREE

VOLCANO

SNOWFLAKES

MOON

CLOUDS

SUN

MOUNTAINS

RIVER

RAIN

RAINBOW

FLOWER

PALM TREE

BENCH

FENCE

SWING

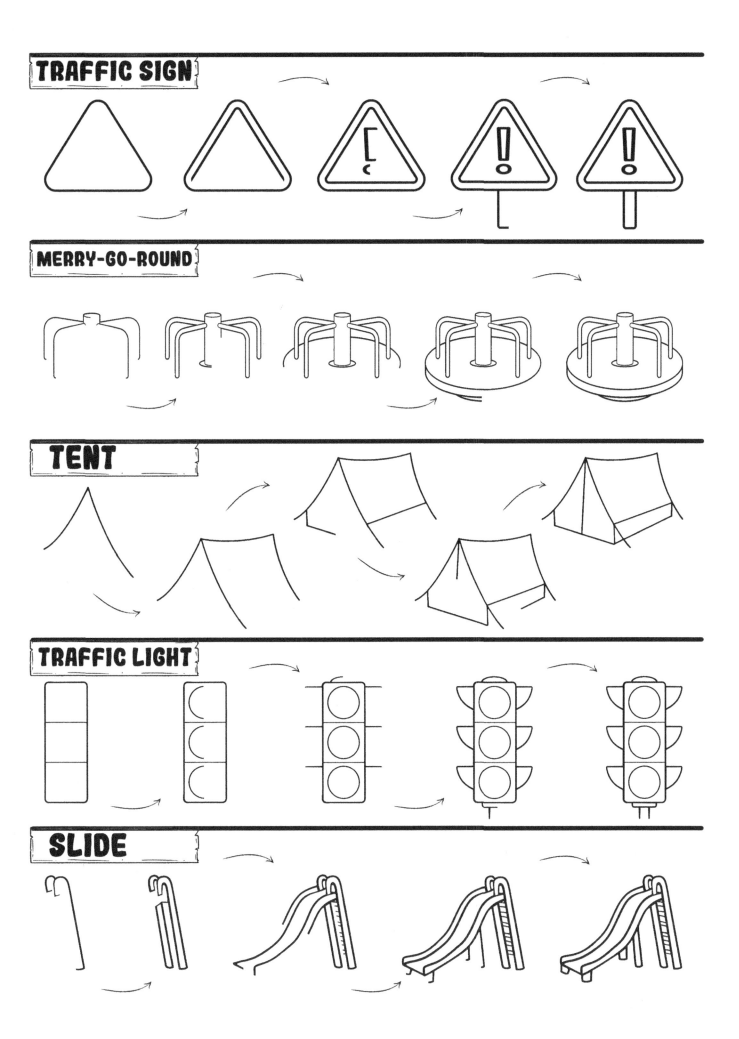

TRAFFIC SIGN

MERRY-GO-ROUND

TENT

TRAFFIC LIGHT

SLIDE

HOUSE

SANDBOX

ZEBRA CROSSING

TRAMPOLINE

SEESAW

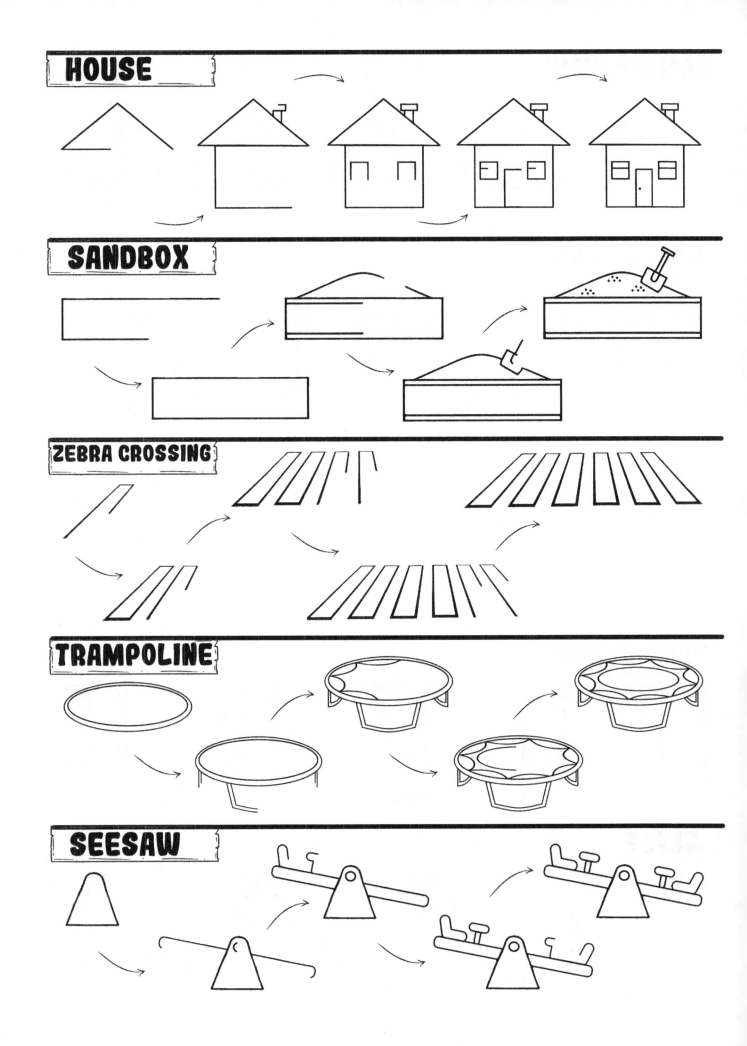

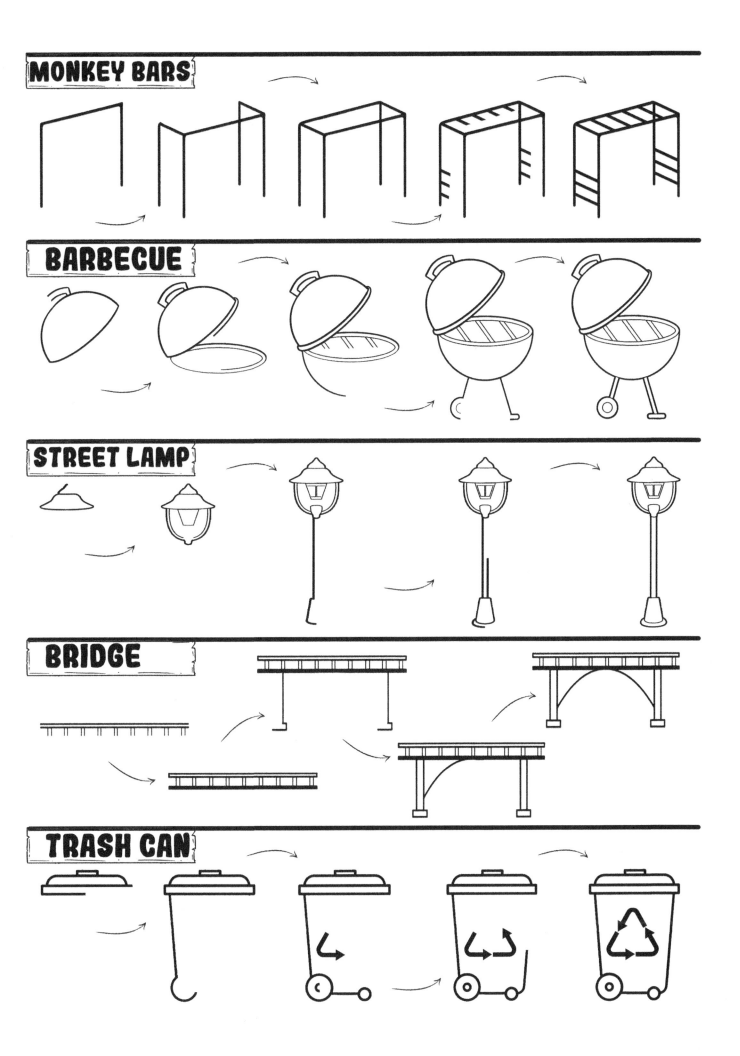

MONKEY BARS

BARBECUE

STREET LAMP

BRIDGE

TRASH CAN

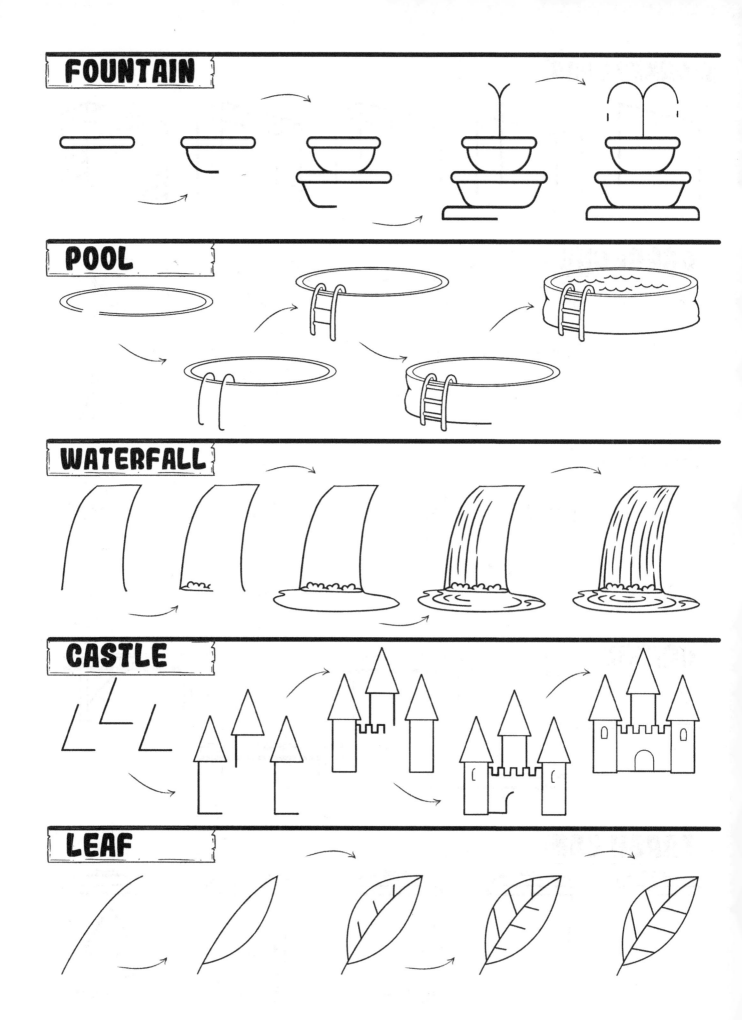

FOUNTAIN

POOL

WATERFALL

CASTLE

LEAF

CHRISTMAS TREE

BUSH

FIRE

PHONE BOOTH

PLANT POT

BIRDHOUSE

FIREWORKS

SHOP

CIRCUS

ROCK

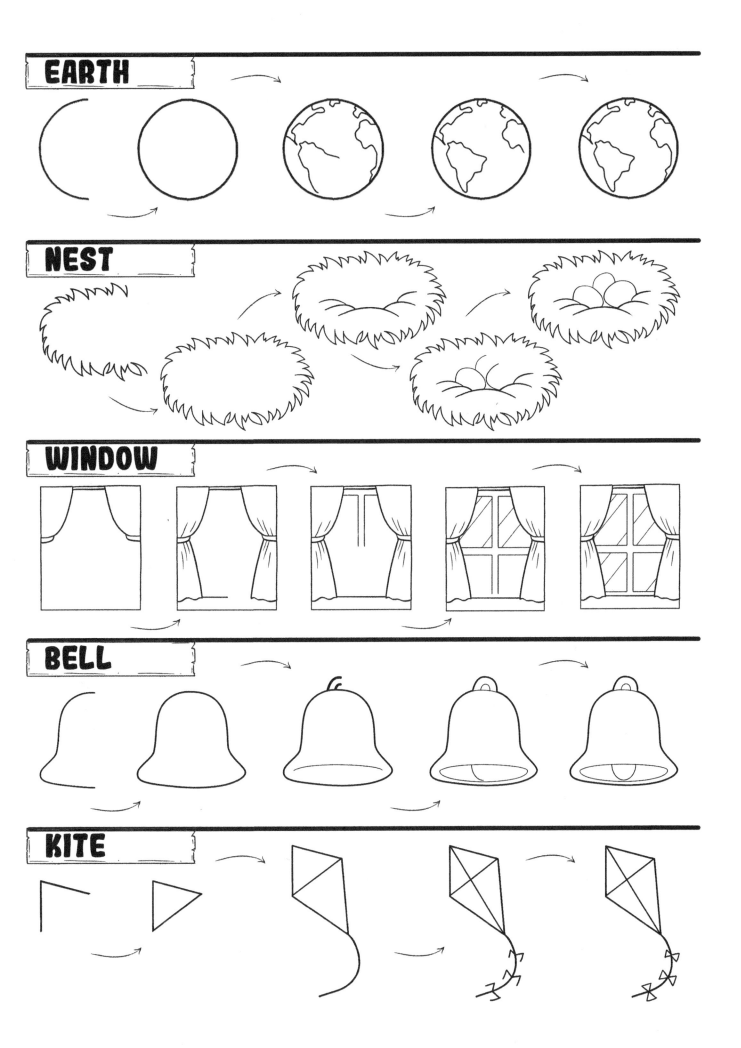

EARTH

NEST

WINDOW

BELL

KITE

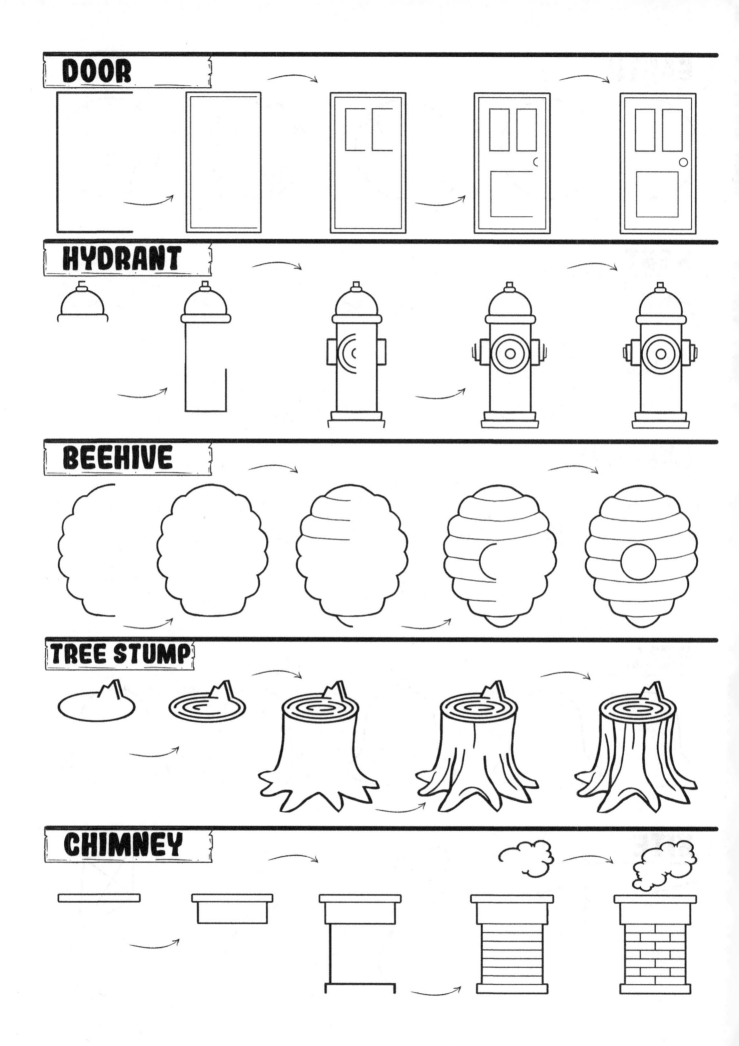

DOOR

HYDRANT

BEEHIVE

TREE STUMP

CHIMNEY

GUITAR

HARP

TRUMPET

DRUM

BANJO

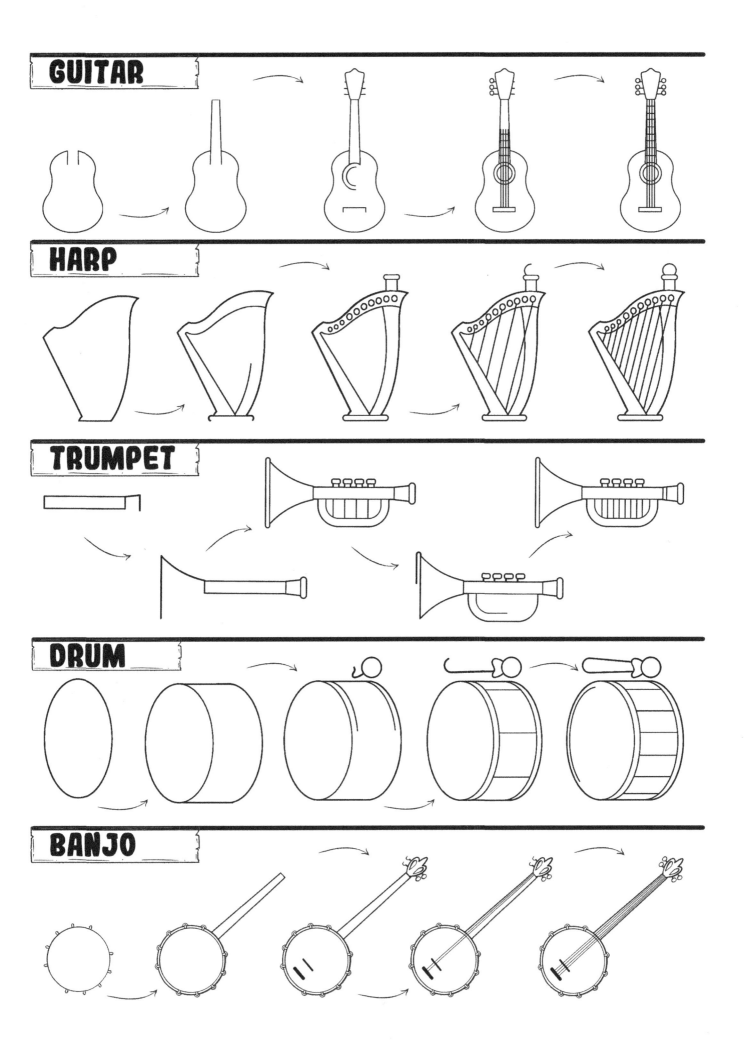

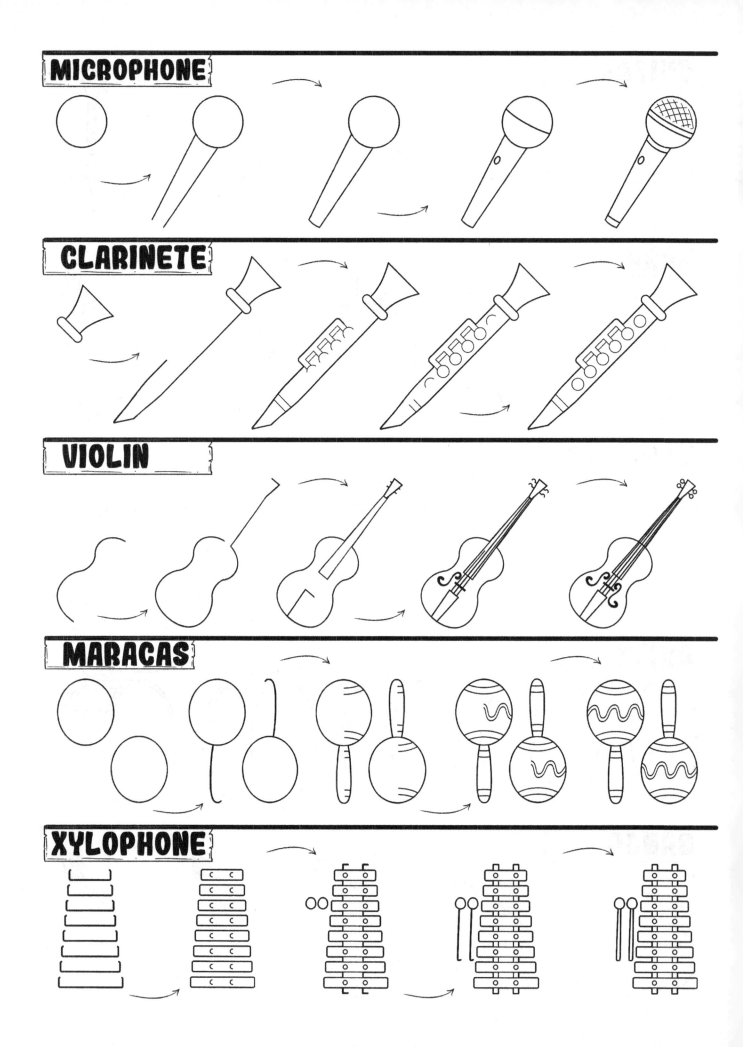

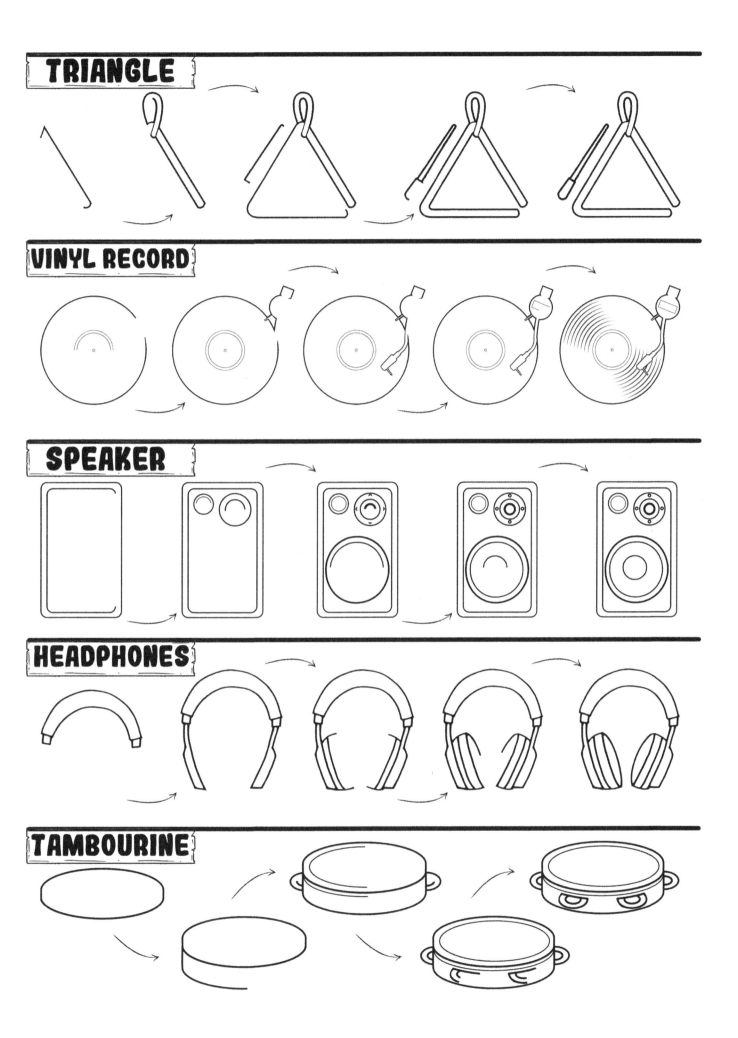

TRIANGLE

VINYL RECORD

SPEAKER

HEADPHONES

TAMBOURINE

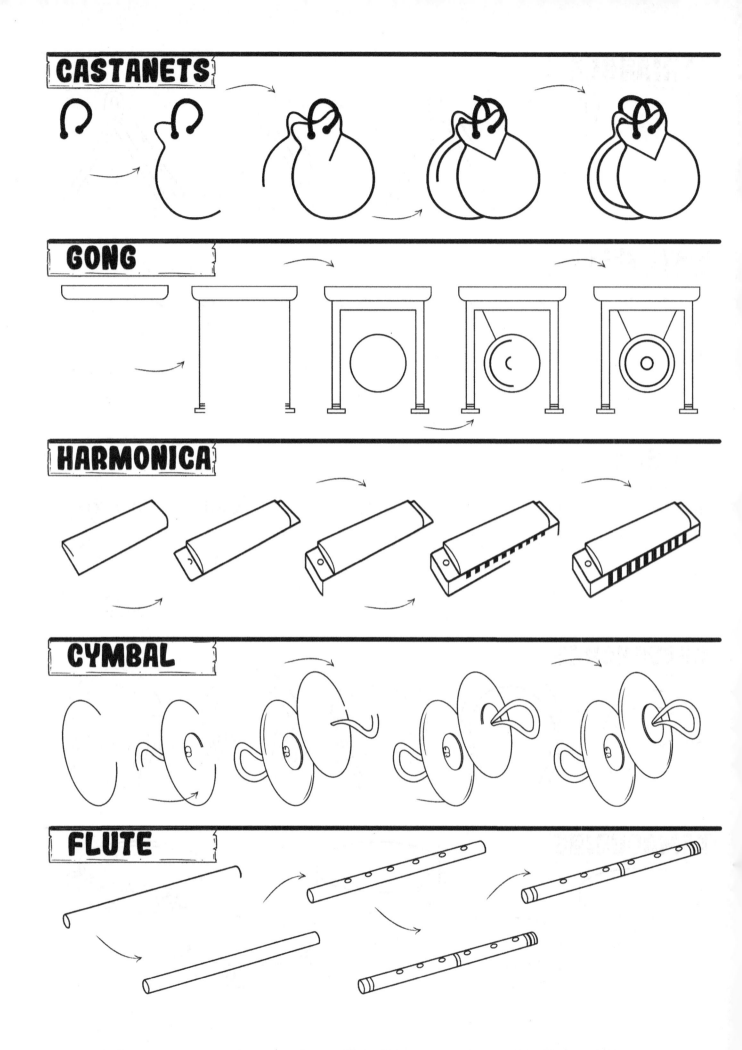

CASTANETS

GONG

HARMONICA

CYMBAL

FLUTE

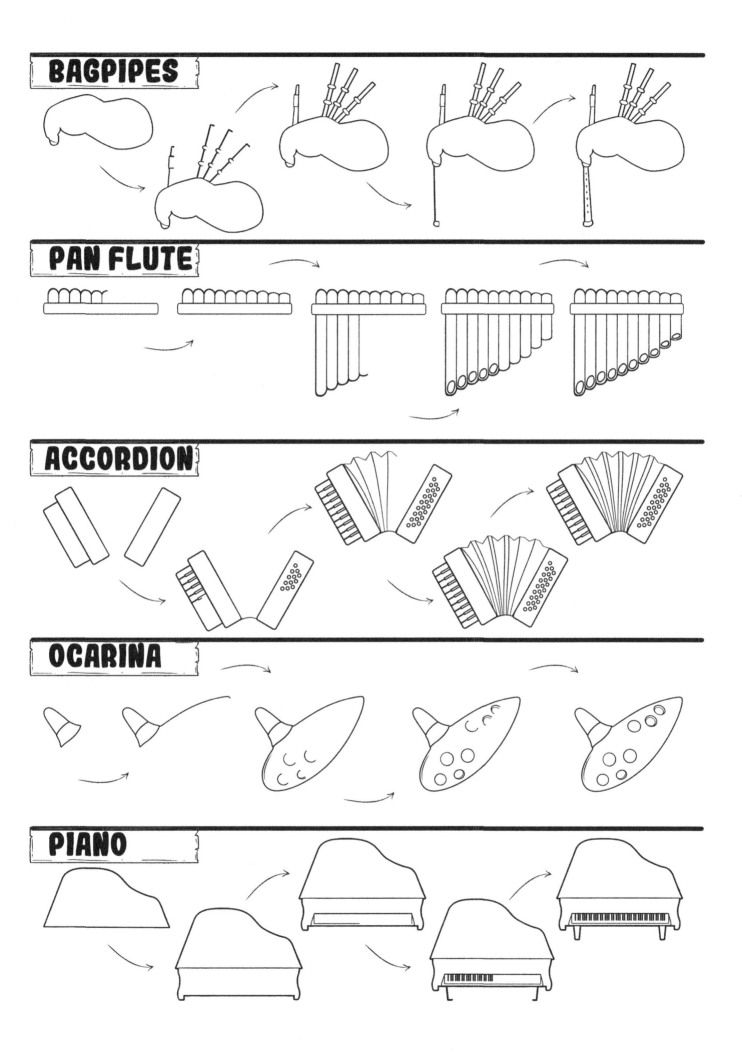

BAGPIPES

PAN FLUTE

ACCORDION

OCARINA

PIANO

METRONOME

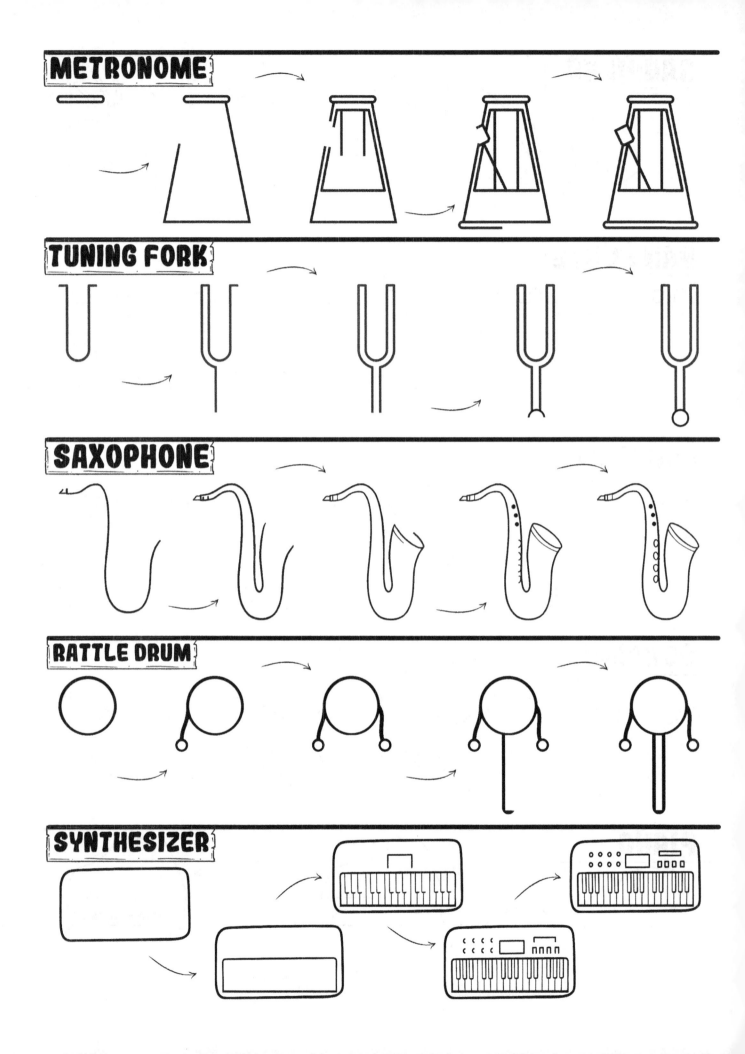

TUNING FORK

SAXOPHONE

RATTLE DRUM

SYNTHESIZER

T-SHIRT

DRESS

GLOVES

SCARF

BASEBALL CAP

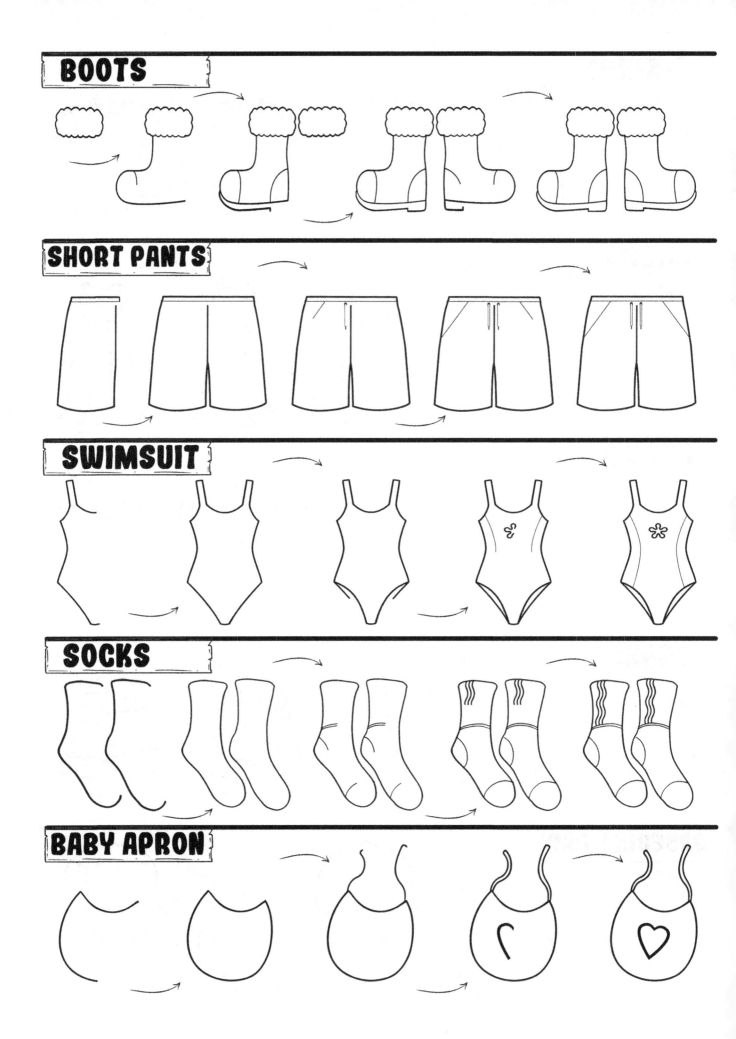

BOOTS

SHORT PANTS

SWIMSUIT

SOCKS

BABY APRON

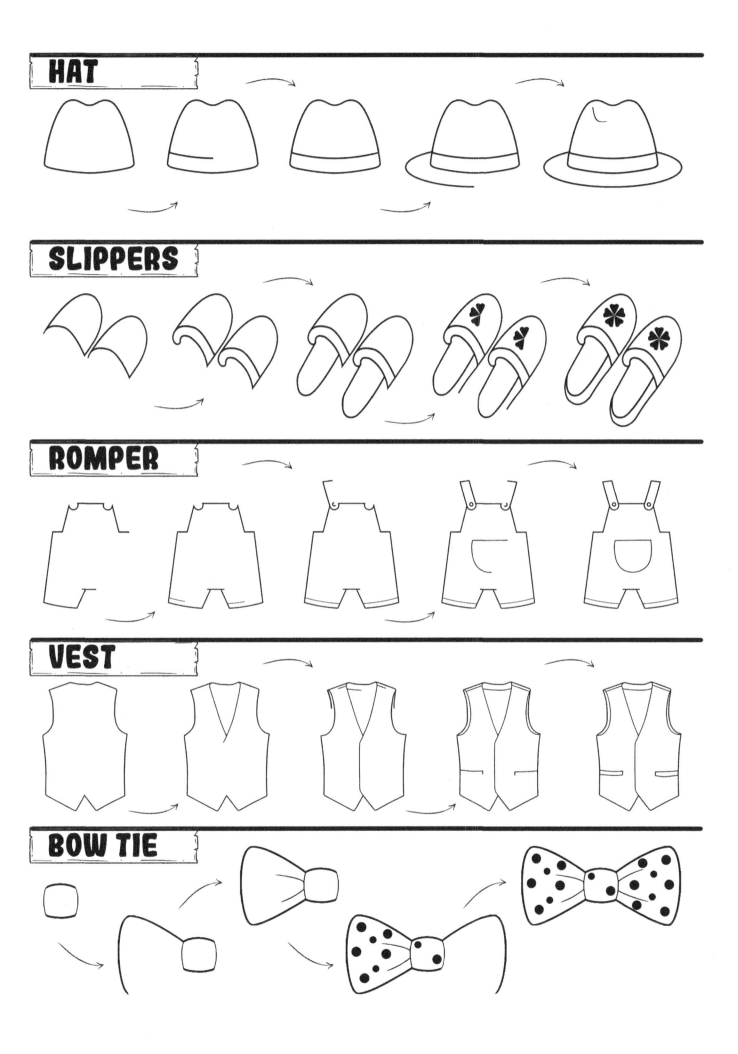

HAT

SLIPPERS

ROMPER

VEST

BOW TIE

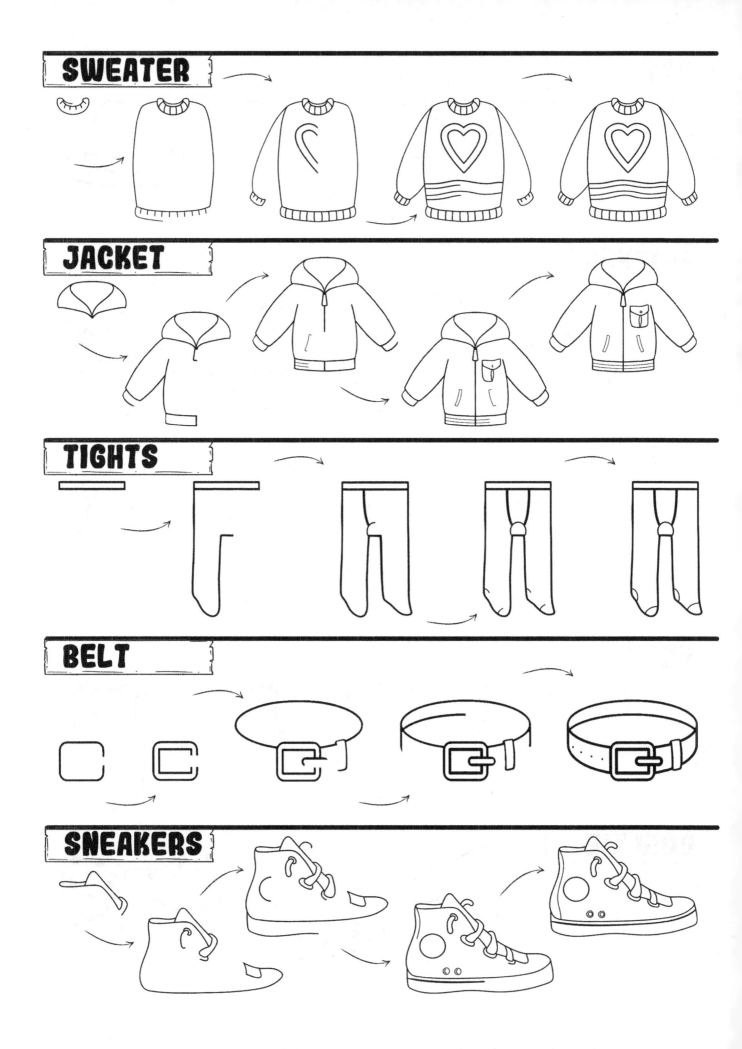

SWEATER

JACKET

TIGHTS

BELT

SNEAKERS

COAT

JEANS

HOODIE

BALL GOWN

SUNGLASSES

HAND BAG

A SKIRT

HIGH HEELS

HAIR BAND

TIE

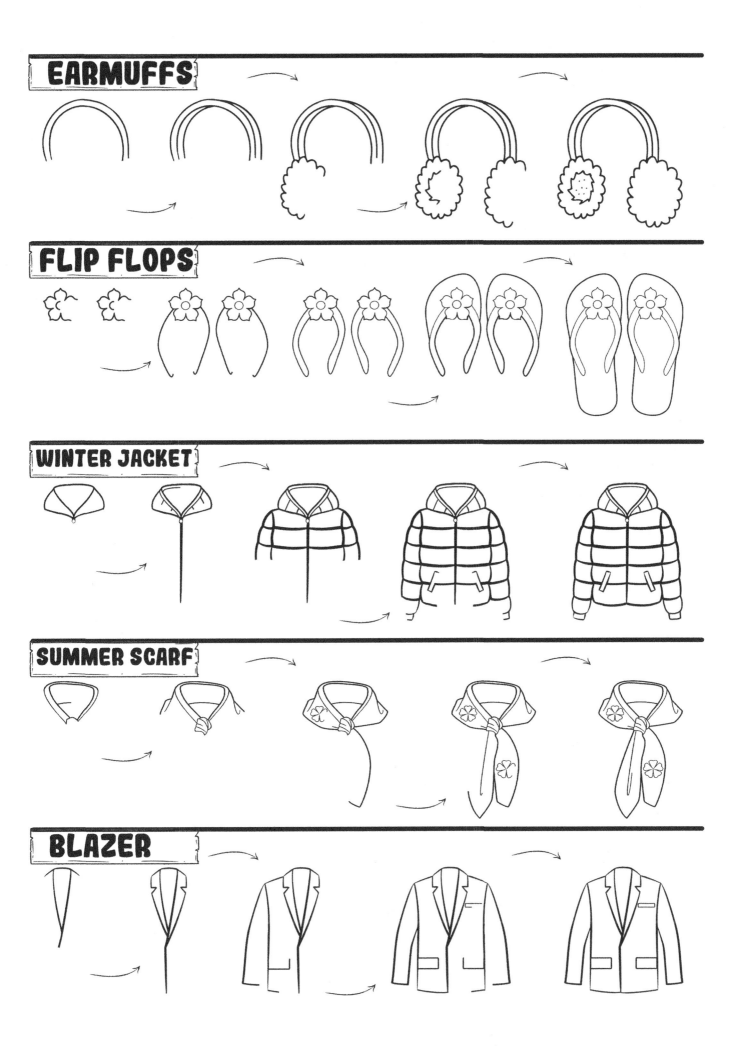

EARMUFFS

FLIP FLOPS

WINTER JACKET

SUMMER SCARF

BLAZER

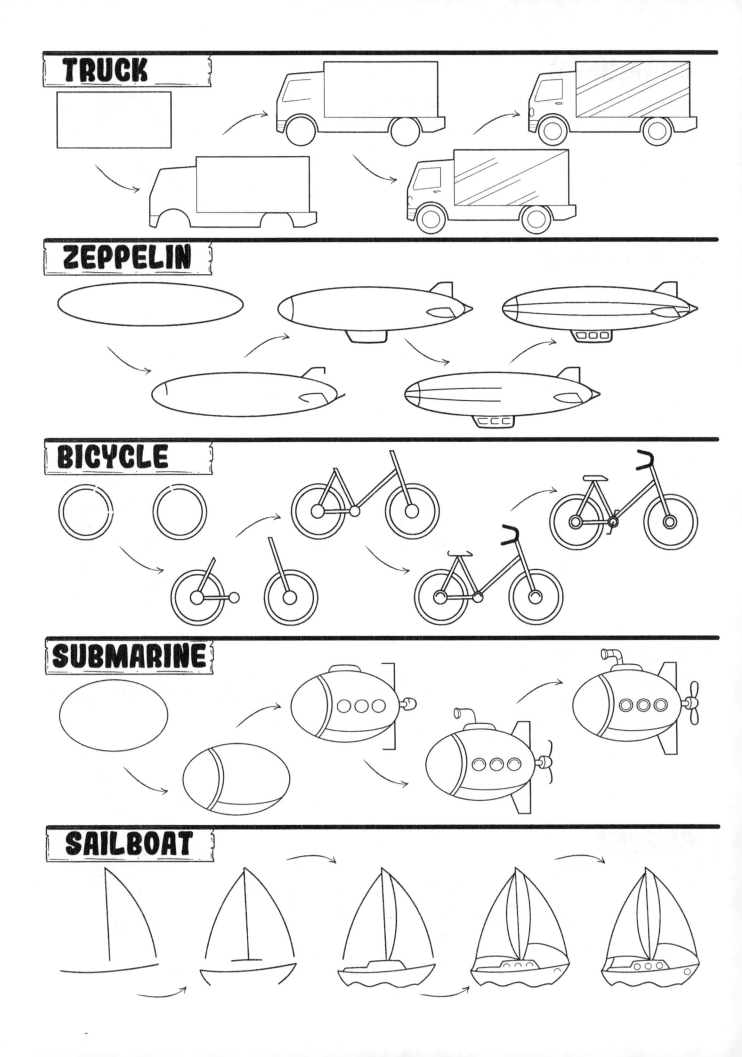

TRUCK

ZEPPELIN

BICYCLE

SUBMARINE

SAILBOAT

AIRPLANE

CAR

TRAIN

BUS

HOT AIR BALLOON

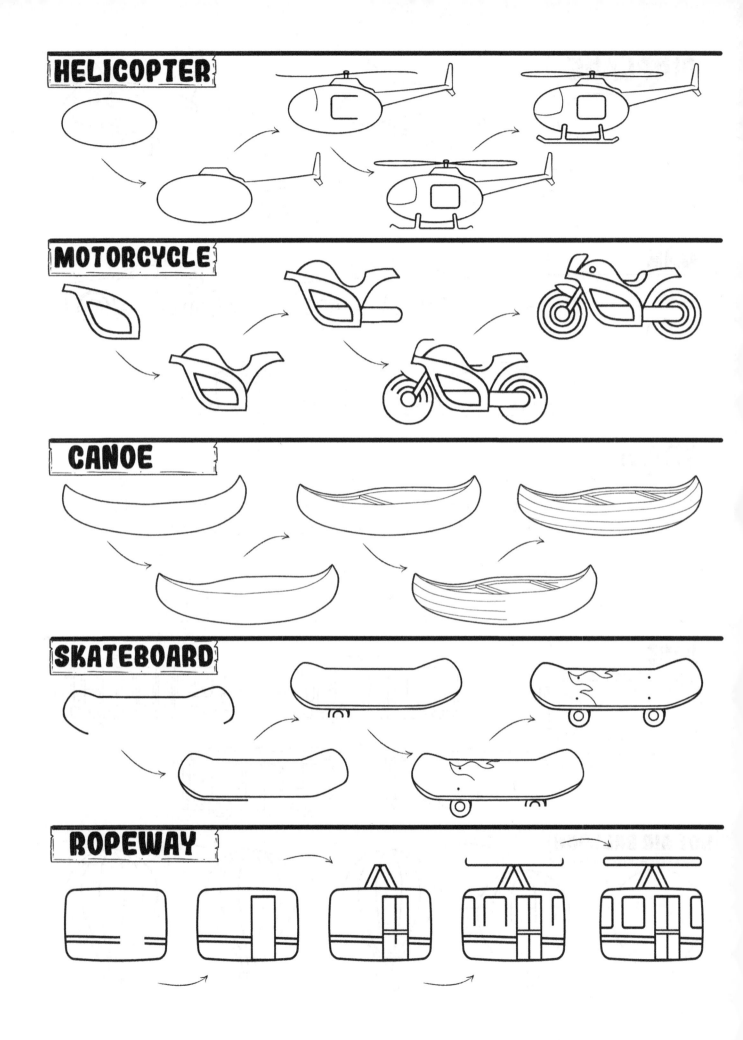

HELICOPTER

MOTORCYCLE

CANOE

SKATEBOARD

ROPEWAY

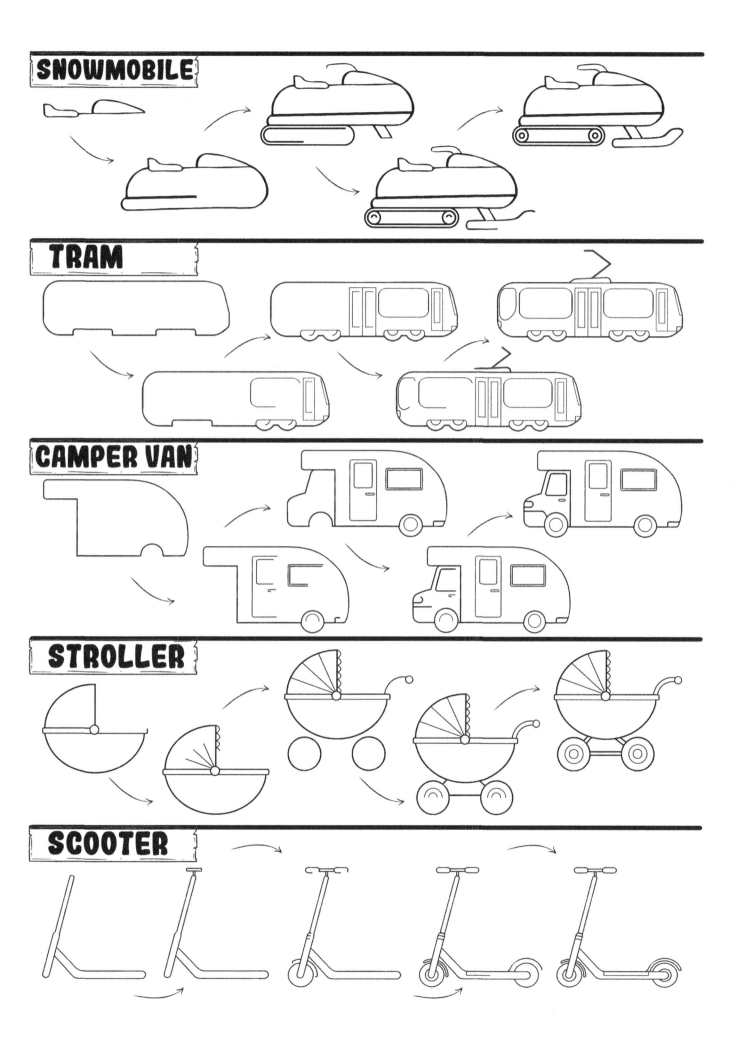

SNOWMOBILE

TRAM

CAMPER VAN

STROLLER

SCOOTER

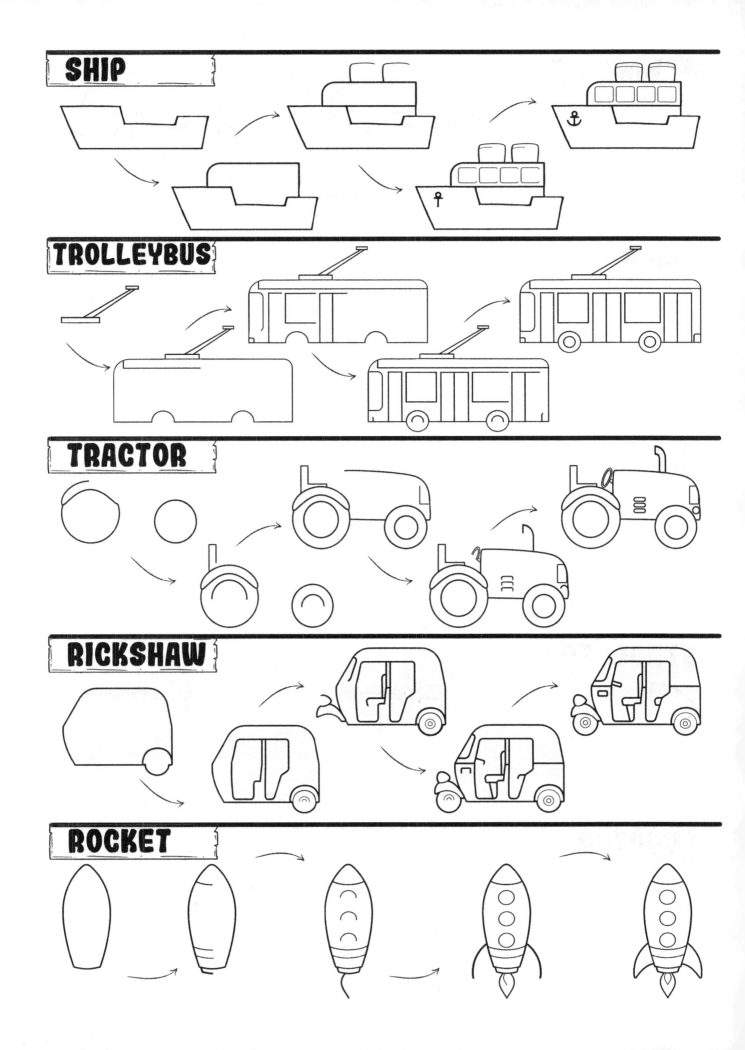

SHIP

TROLLEYBUS

TRACTOR

RICKSHAW

ROCKET

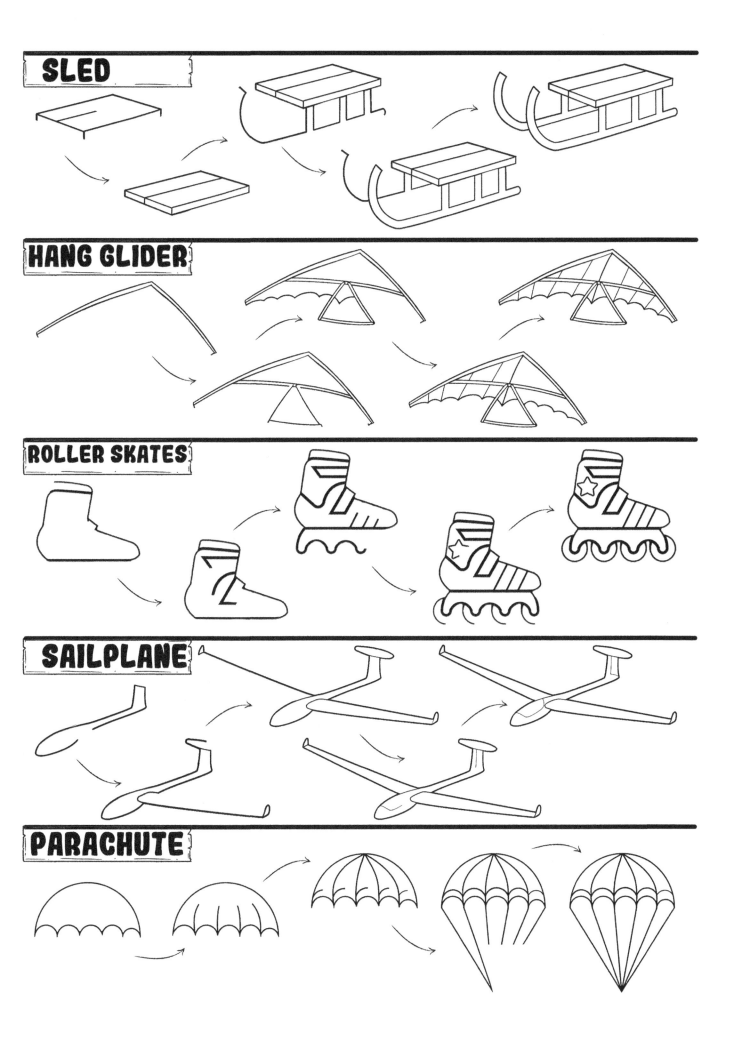

SLED

HANG GLIDER

ROLLER SKATES

SAILPLANE

PARACHUTE

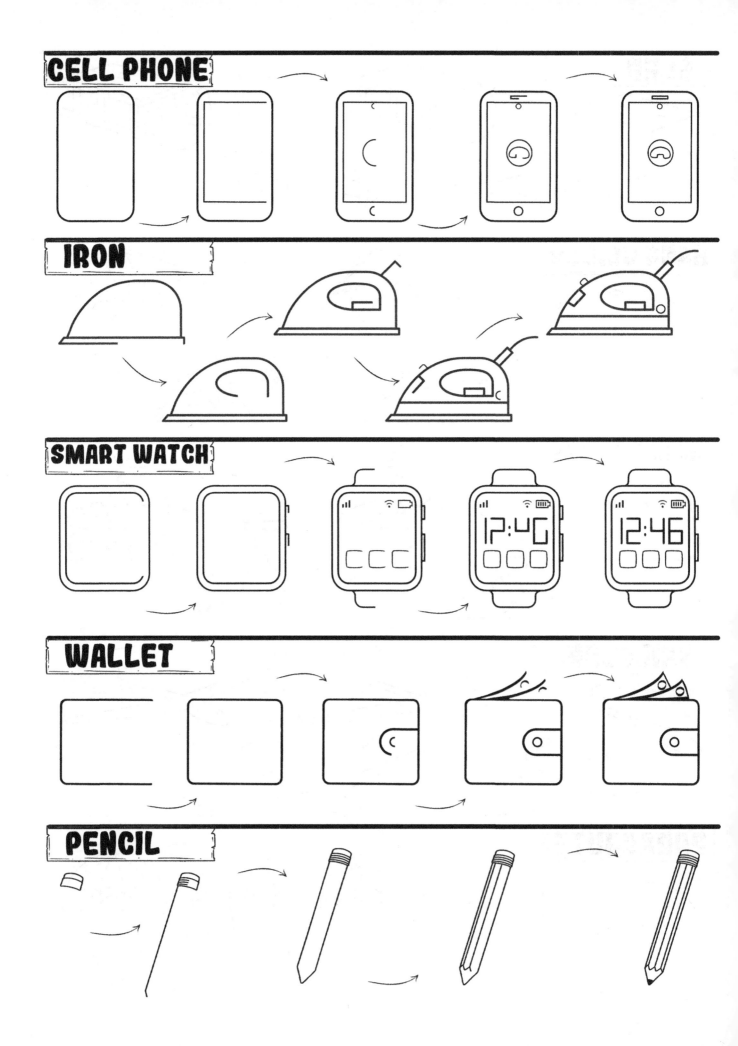

CELL PHONE

IRON

SMART WATCH

WALLET

PENCIL

SCISSORS

OVEN MITT

PILLOW

PAINT PALLETE

BOOK

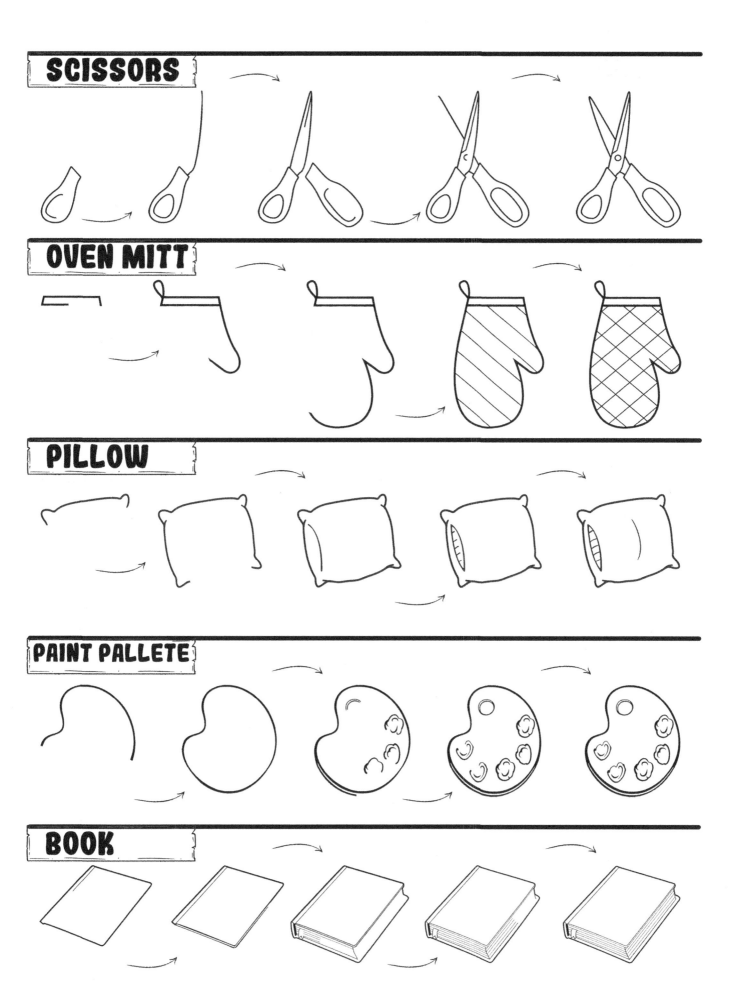

FLOWER POT

BALL

SKILLET

SPOON

BALLOON

POT

FORK

TEAPOT

GLASS

BOWL

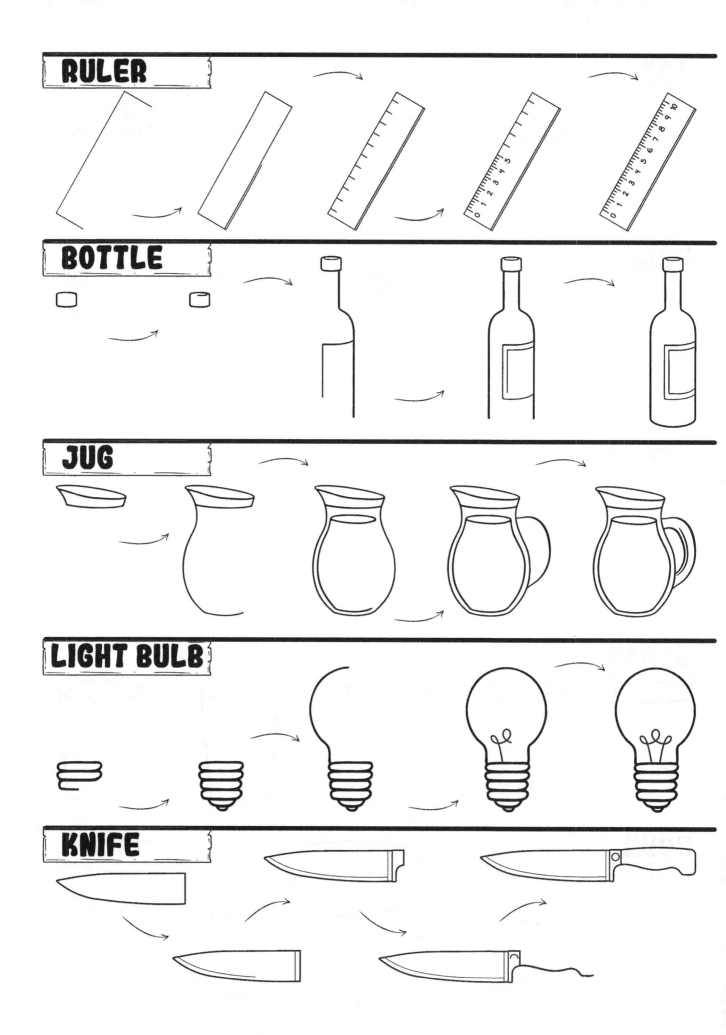

RULER

BOTTLE

JUG

LIGHT BULB

KNIFE

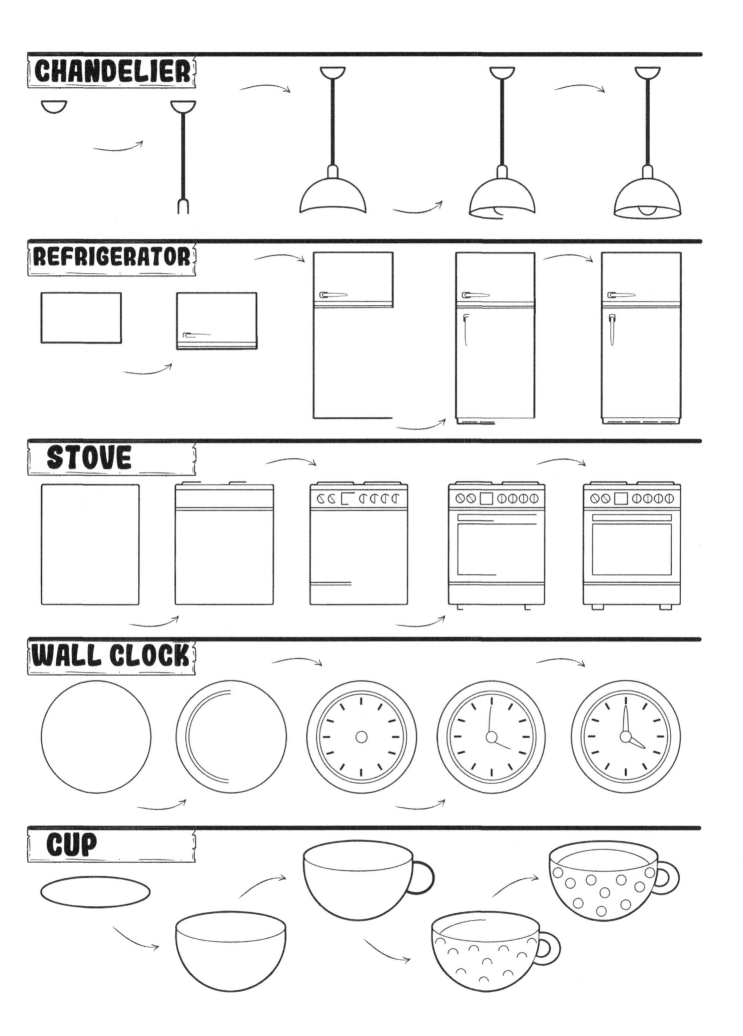

CHANDELIER

REFRIGERATOR

STOVE

WALL CLOCK

CUP

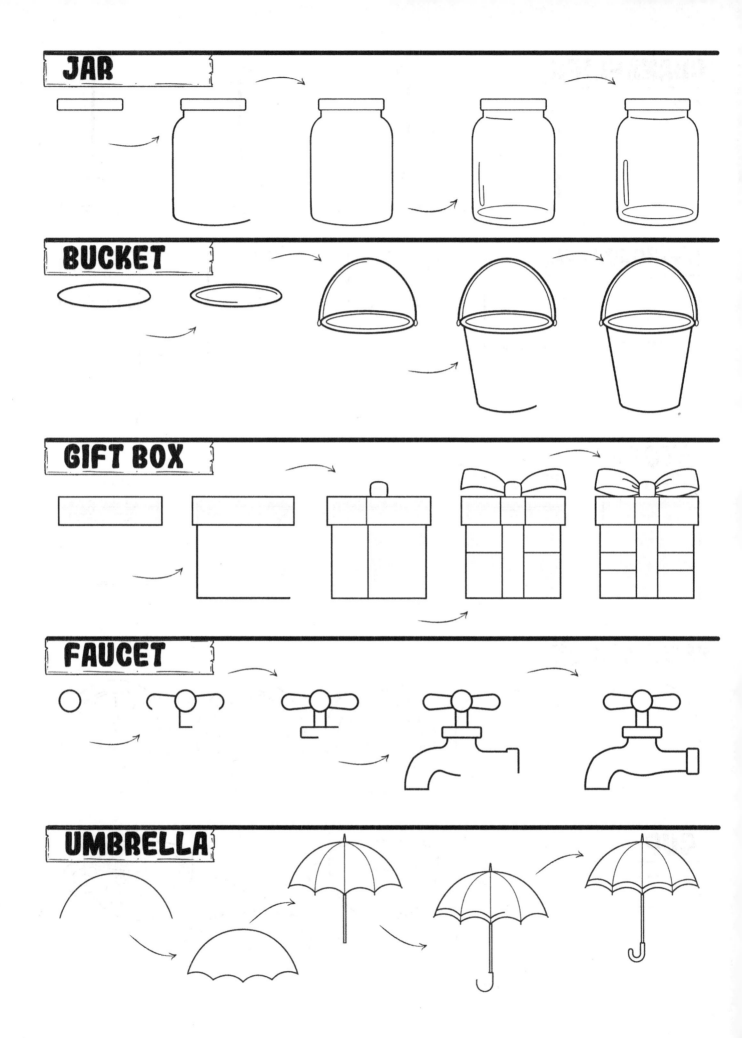

JAR

BUCKET

GIFT BOX

FAUCET

UMBRELLA

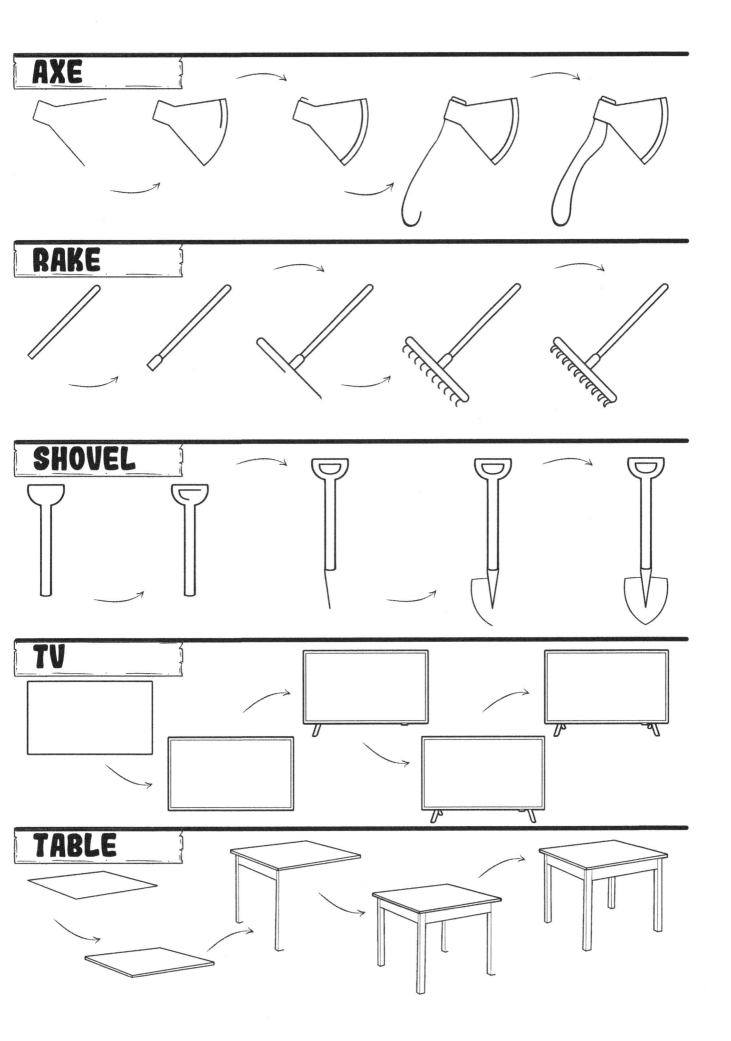

AXE

RAKE

SHOVEL

TV

TABLE

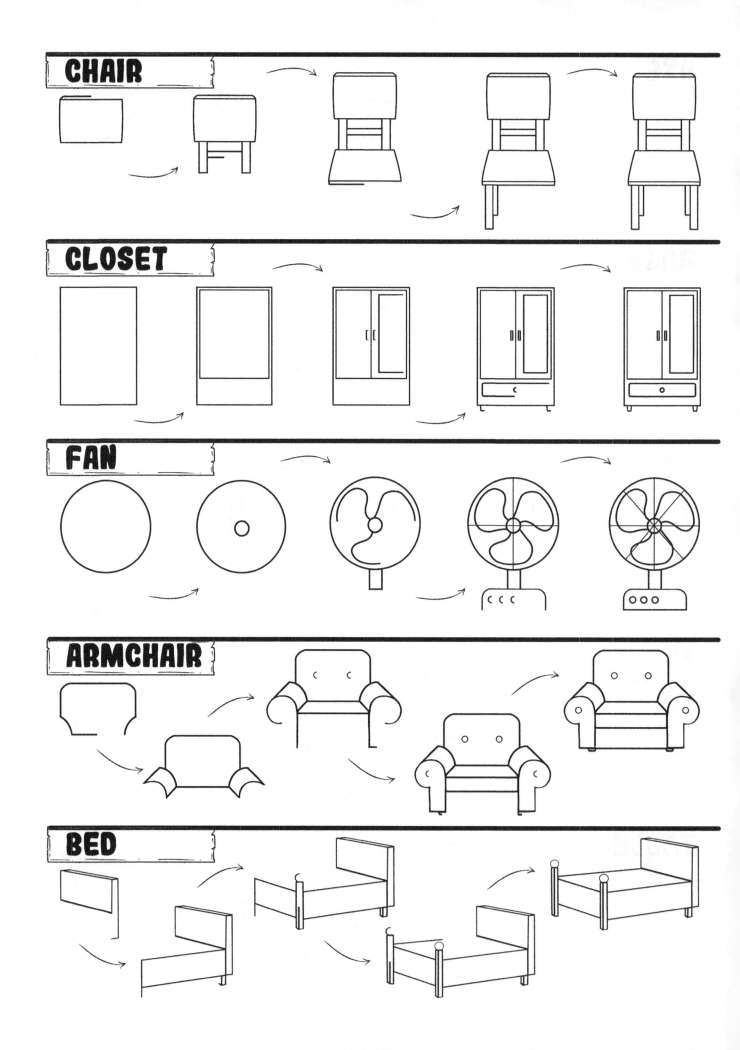

CHAIR

CLOSET

FAN

ARMCHAIR

BED

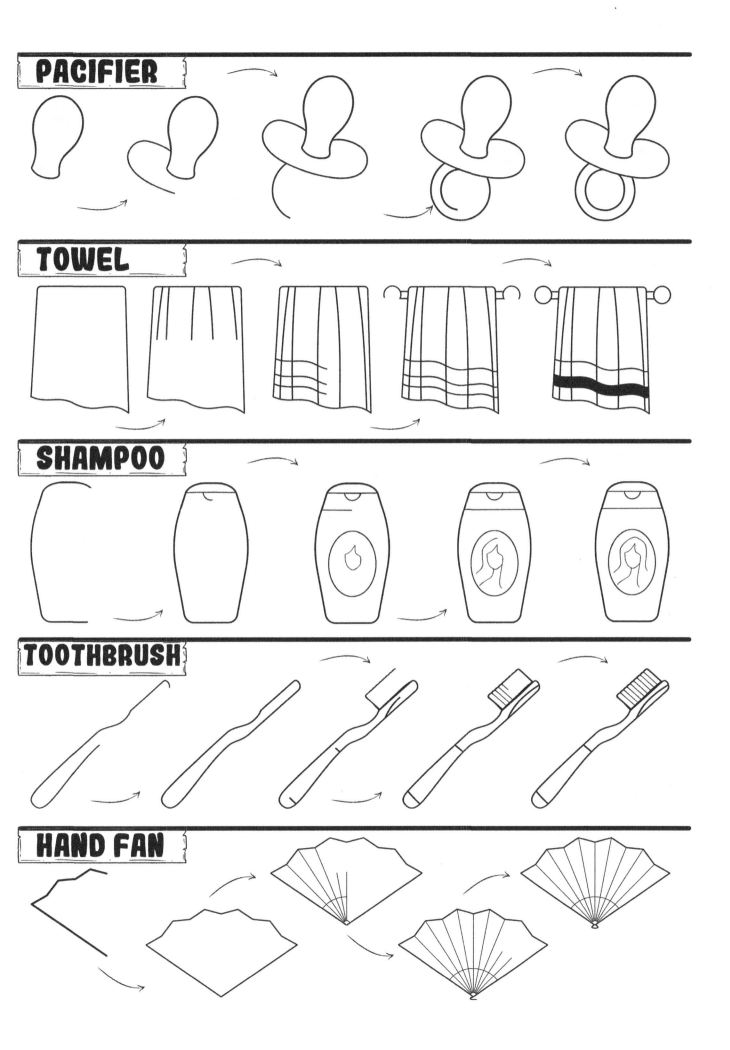

PACIFIER

TOWEL

SHAMPOO

TOOTHBRUSH

HAND FAN

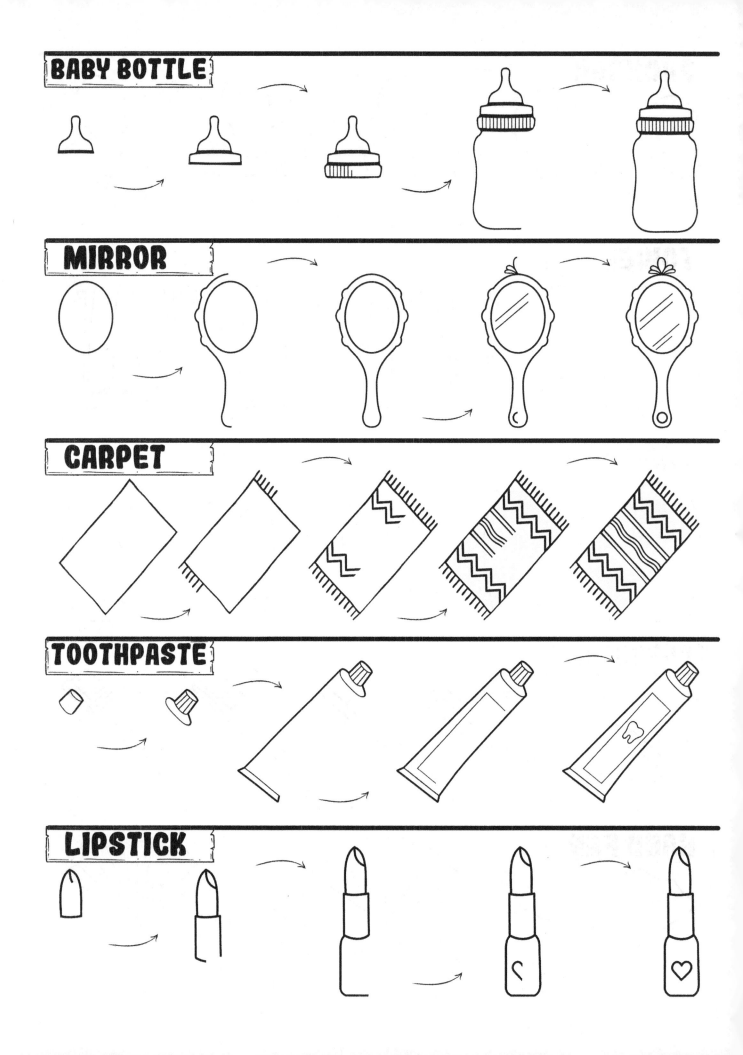

BABY BOTTLE

MIRROR

CARPET

TOOTHPASTE

LIPSTICK

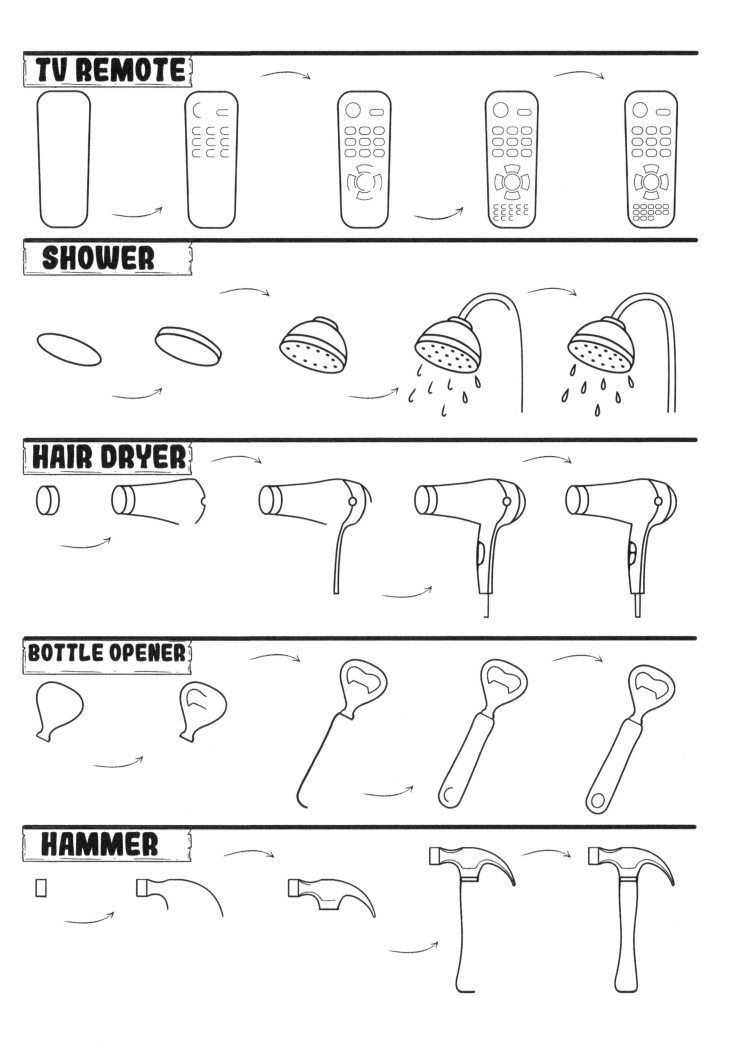

TV REMOTE

SHOWER

HAIR DRYER

BOTTLE OPENER

HAMMER

KEY

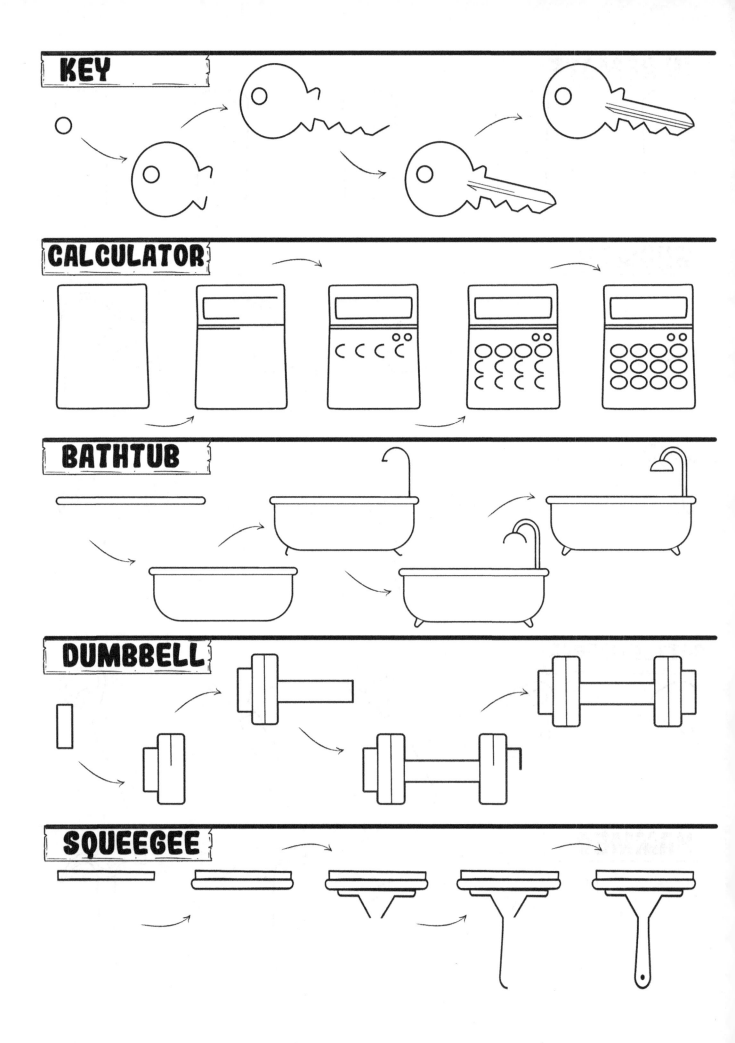

CALCULATOR

BATHTUB

DUMBBELL

SQUEEGEE

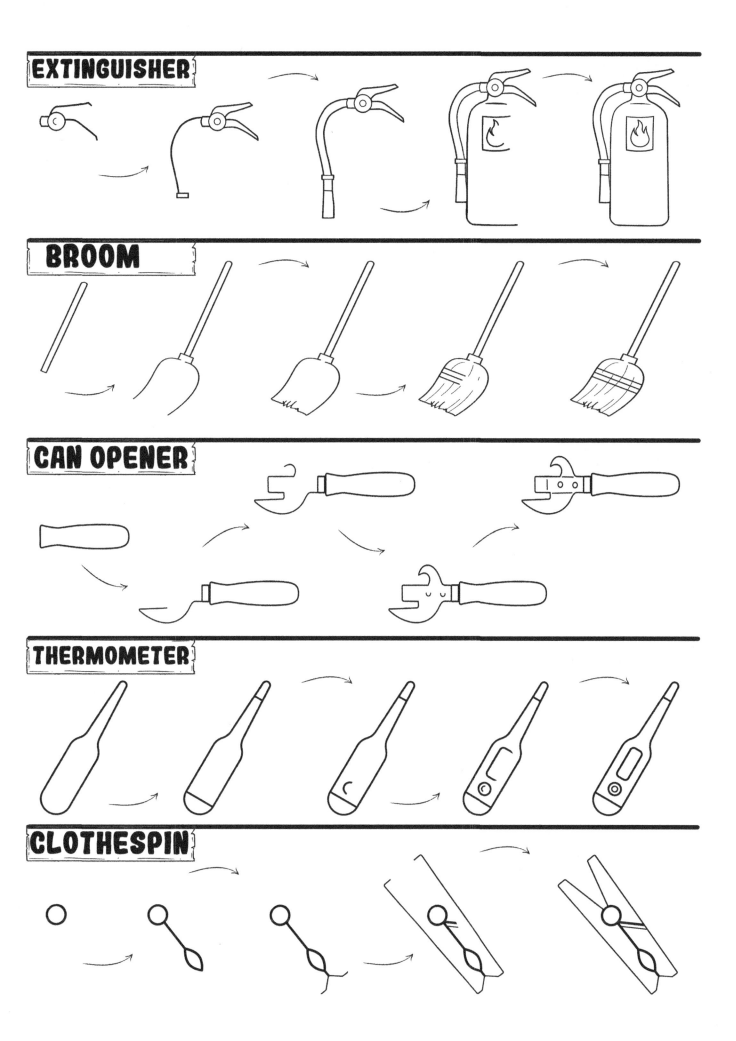

EXTINGUISHER

BROOM

CAN OPENER

THERMOMETER

CLOTHESPIN

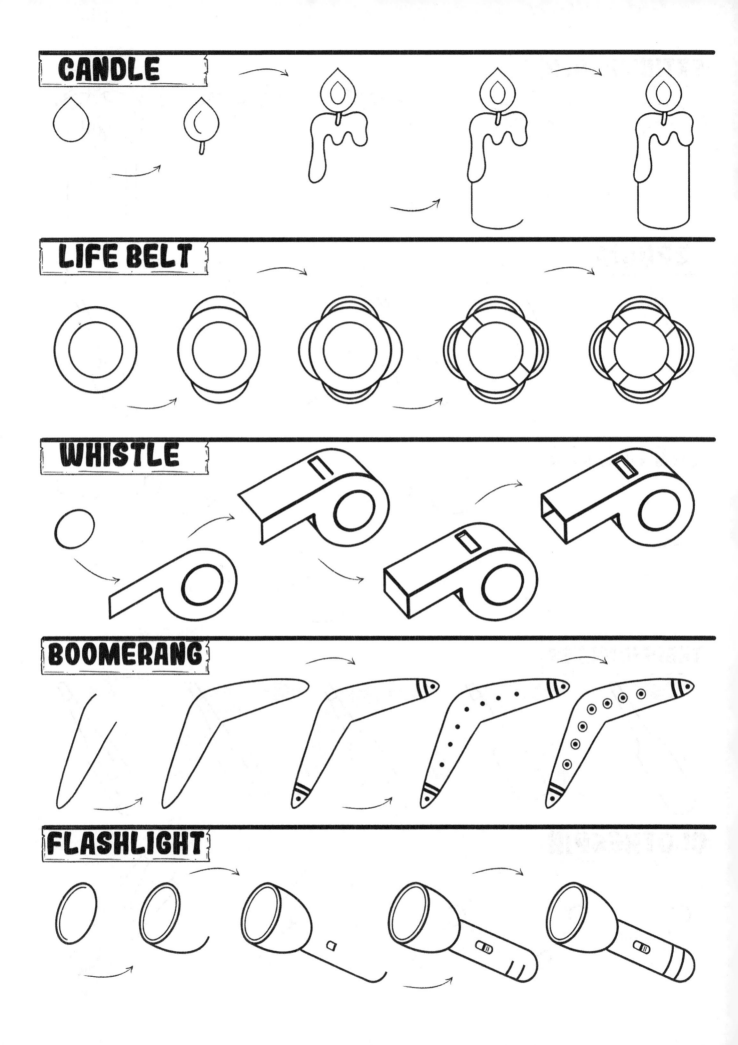

CANDLE

LIFE BELT

WHISTLE

BOOMERANG

FLASHLIGHT

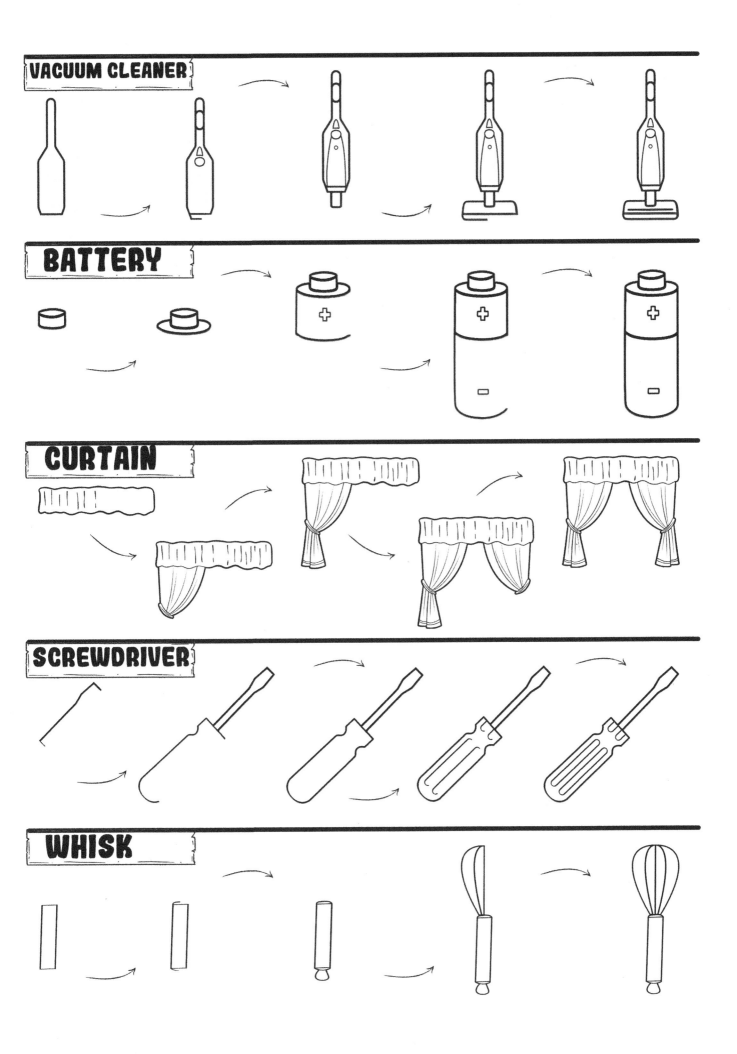

VACUUM CLEANER

BATTERY

CURTAIN

SCREWDRIVER

WHISK

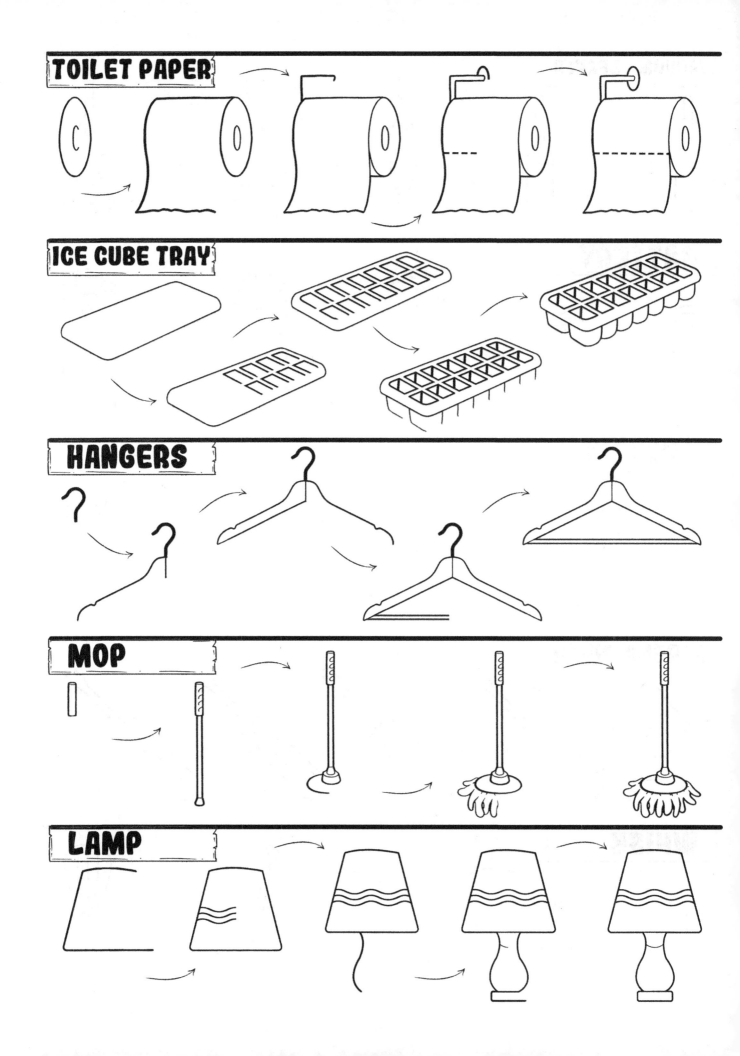

TOILET PAPER

ICE CUBE TRAY

HANGERS

MOP

LAMP

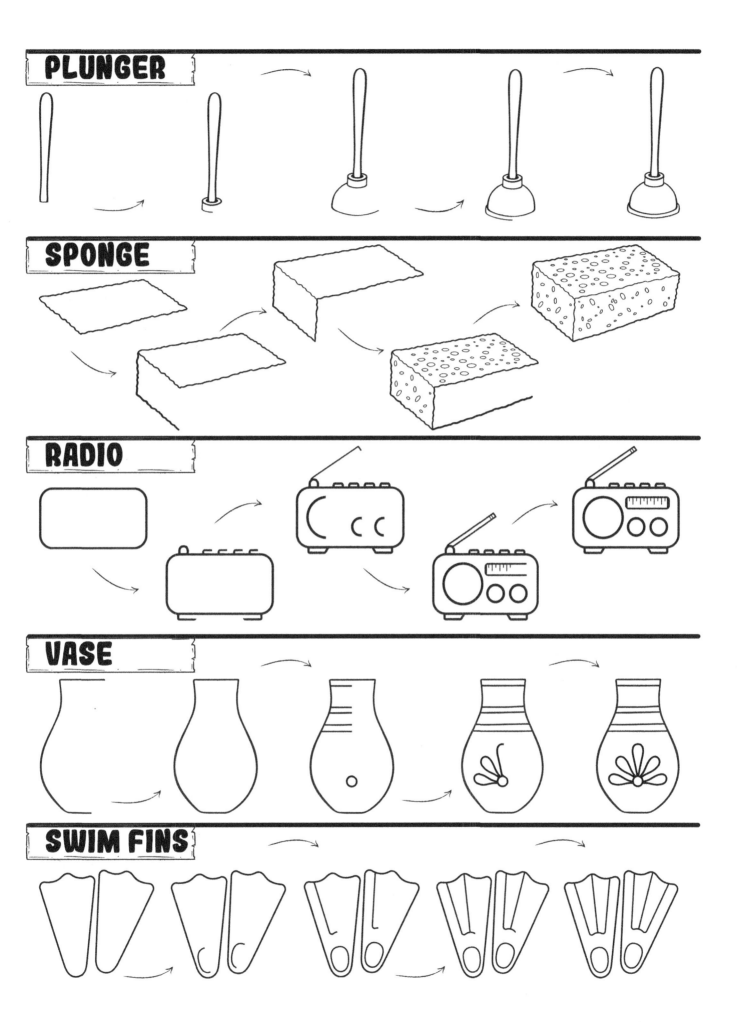

PLUNGER

SPONGE

RADIO

VASE

SWIM FINS

XMAS STOCKING

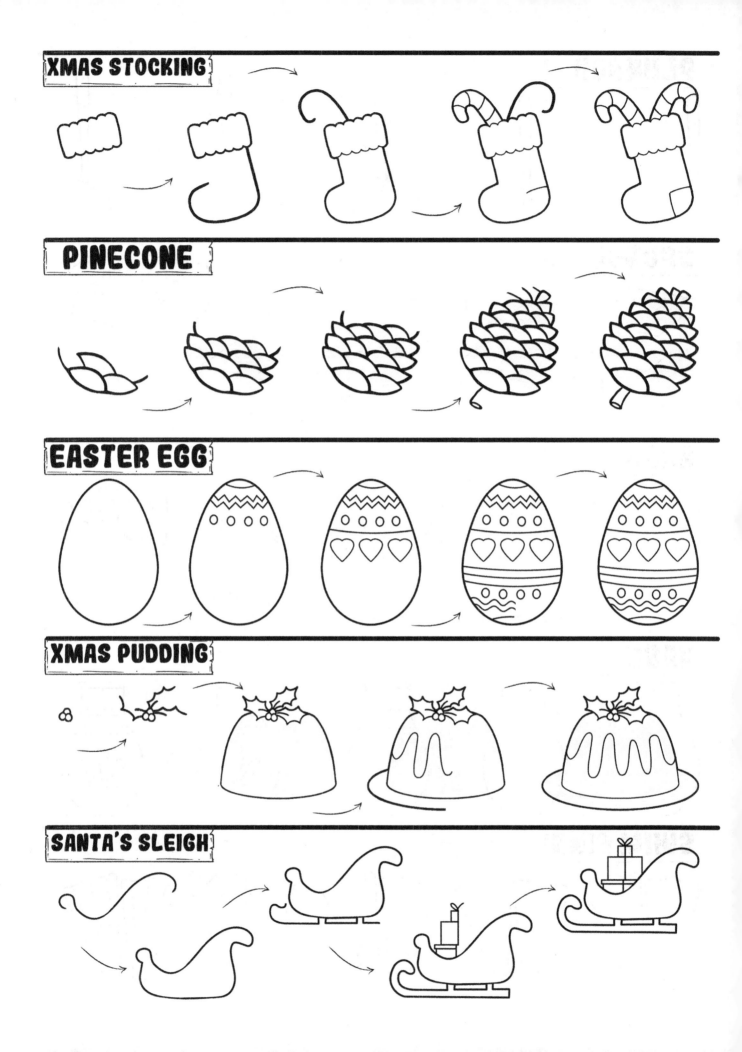

PINECONE

EASTER EGG

XMAS PUDDING

SANTA'S SLEIGH

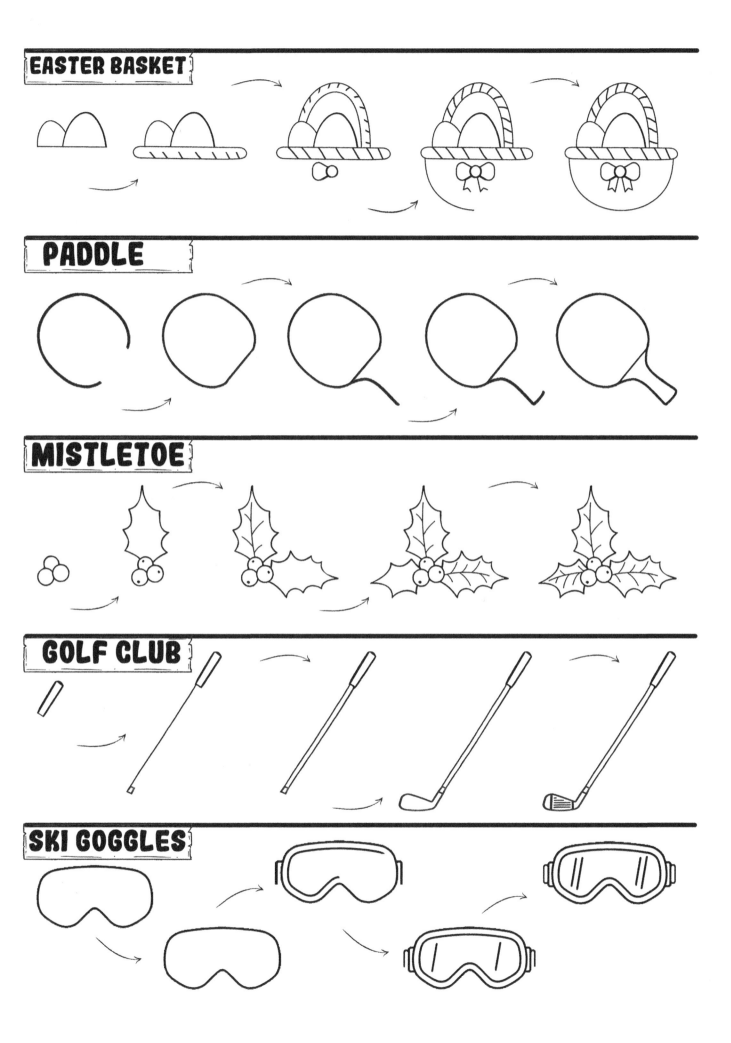

EASTER BASKET

PADDLE

MISTLETOE

GOLF CLUB

SKI GOGGLES

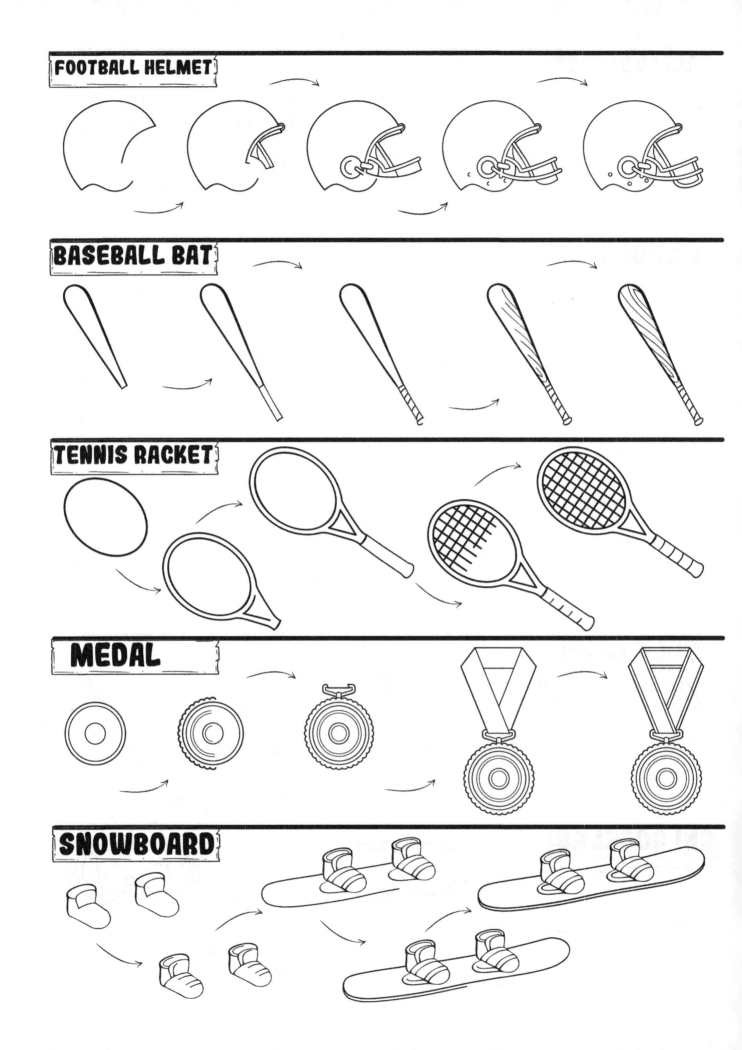

FOOTBALL HELMET

BASEBALL BAT

TENNIS RACKET

MEDAL

SNOWBOARD

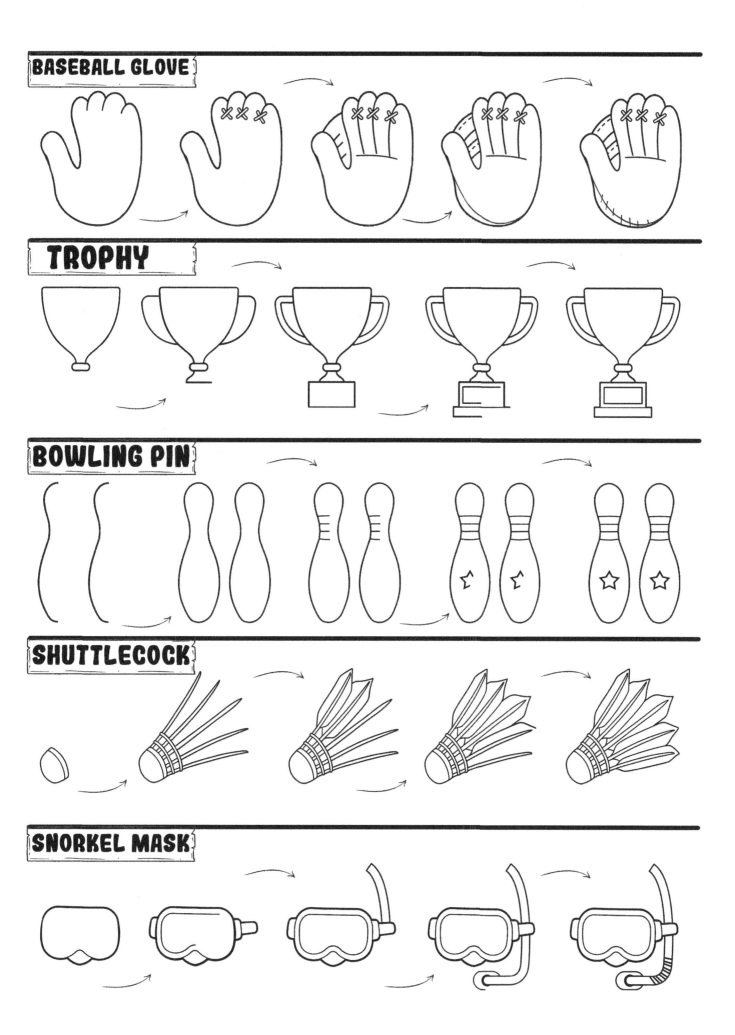

BASEBALL GLOVE

TROPHY

BOWLING PIN

SHUTTLECOCK

SNORKEL MASK

ICE SKATE

BOXING GLOVES

BASKETBALL HOOP

DARTS

FOOTBALL BOOTS

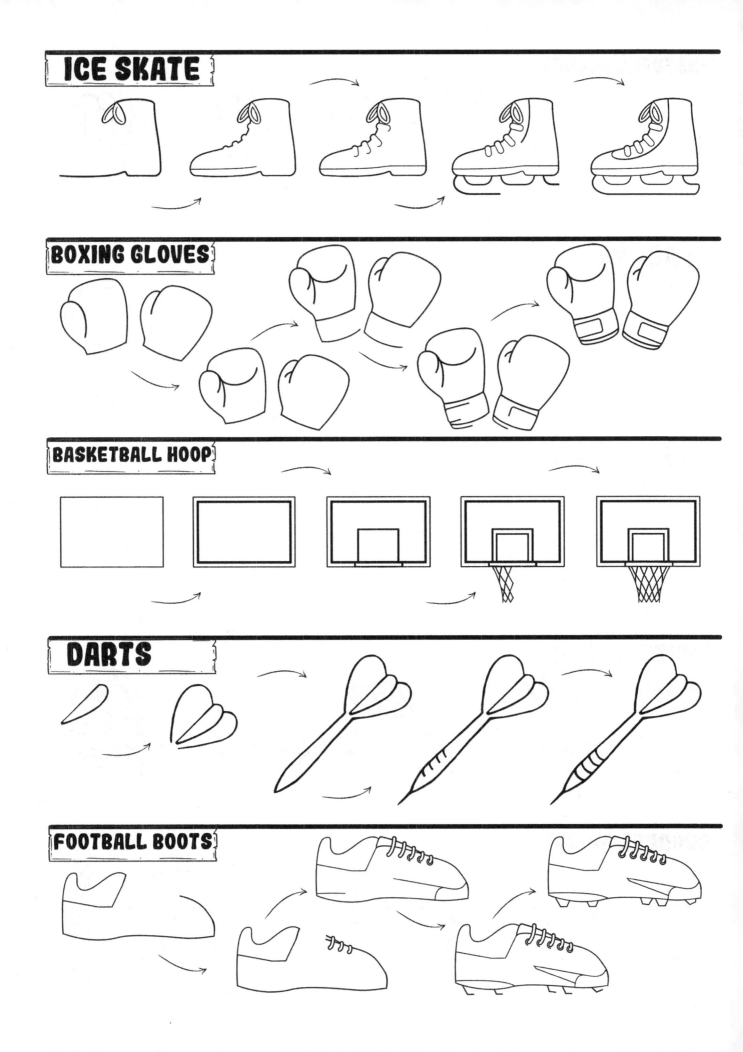

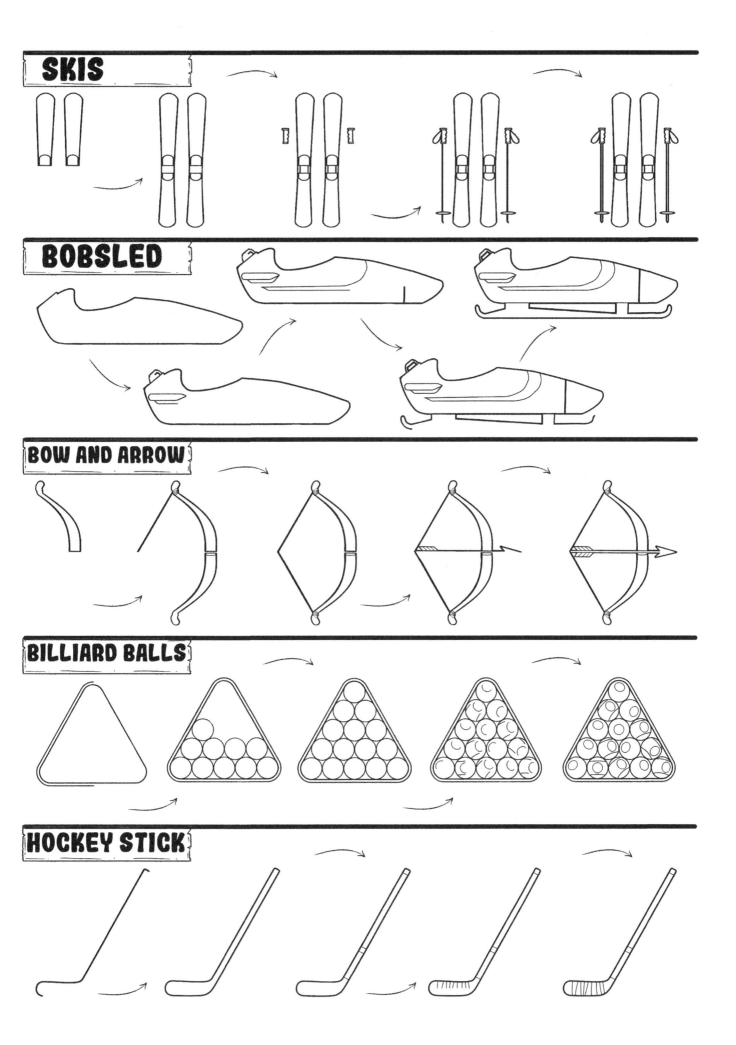

SKIS

BOBSLED

BOW AND ARROW

BILLIARD BALLS

HOCKEY STICK

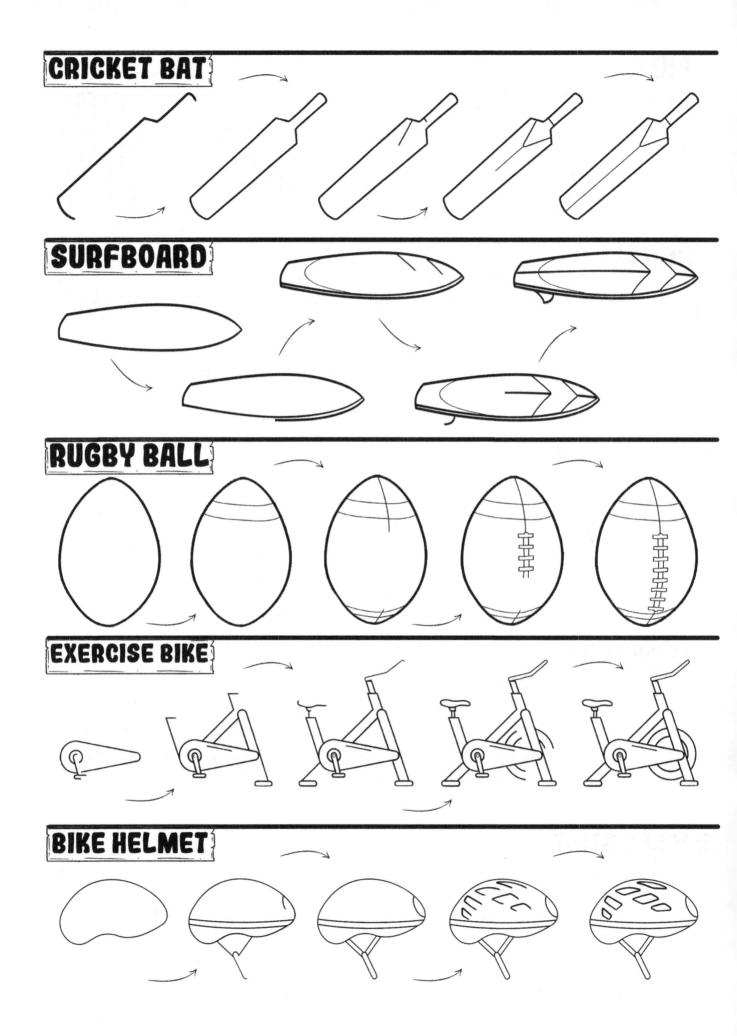

CRICKET BAT

SURFBOARD

RUGBY BALL

EXERCISE BIKE

BIKE HELMET

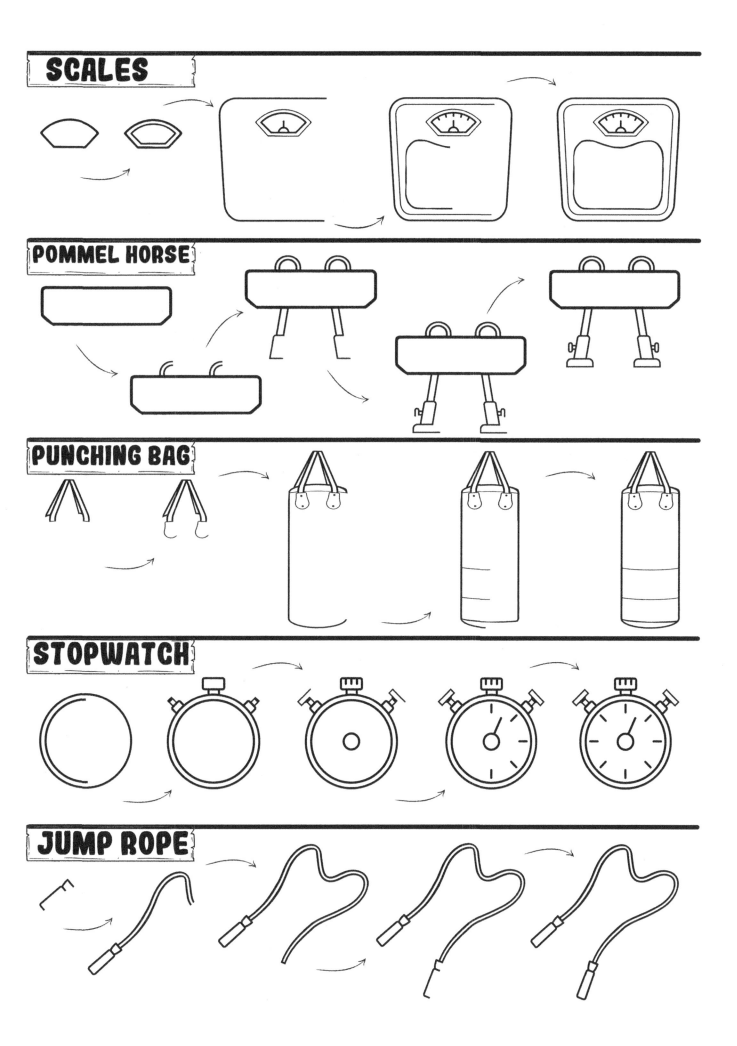

SCALES

POMMEL HORSE

PUNCHING BAG

STOPWATCH

JUMP ROPE

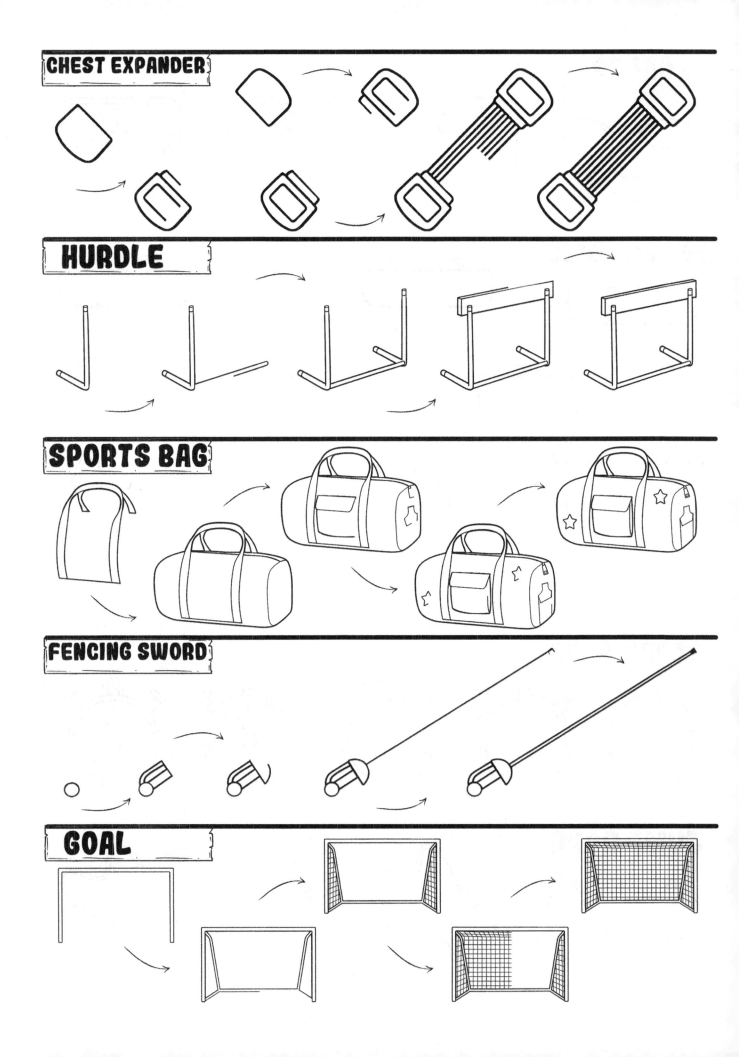

CHEST EXPANDER

HURDLE

SPORTS BAG

FENCING SWORD

GOAL

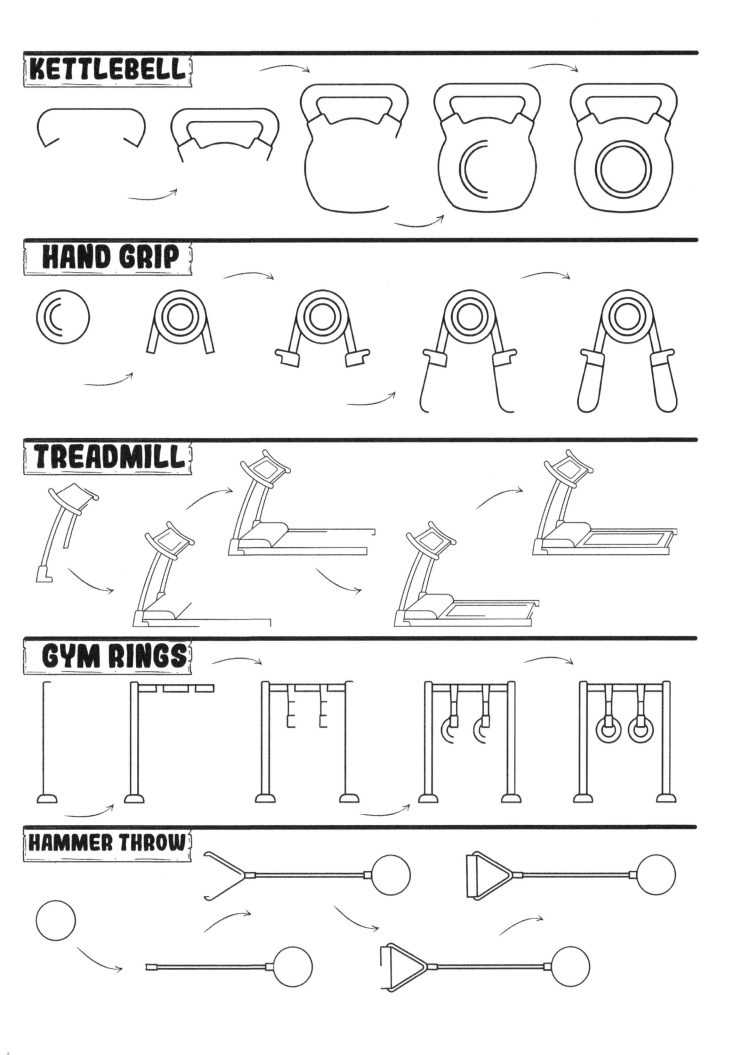

KETTLEBELL

HAND GRIP

TREADMILL

GYM RINGS

HAMMER THROW

ICE AXE

FISHING ROD

WATER POLO CAP

CROQUET MALLET

SPORTS BOTTLE

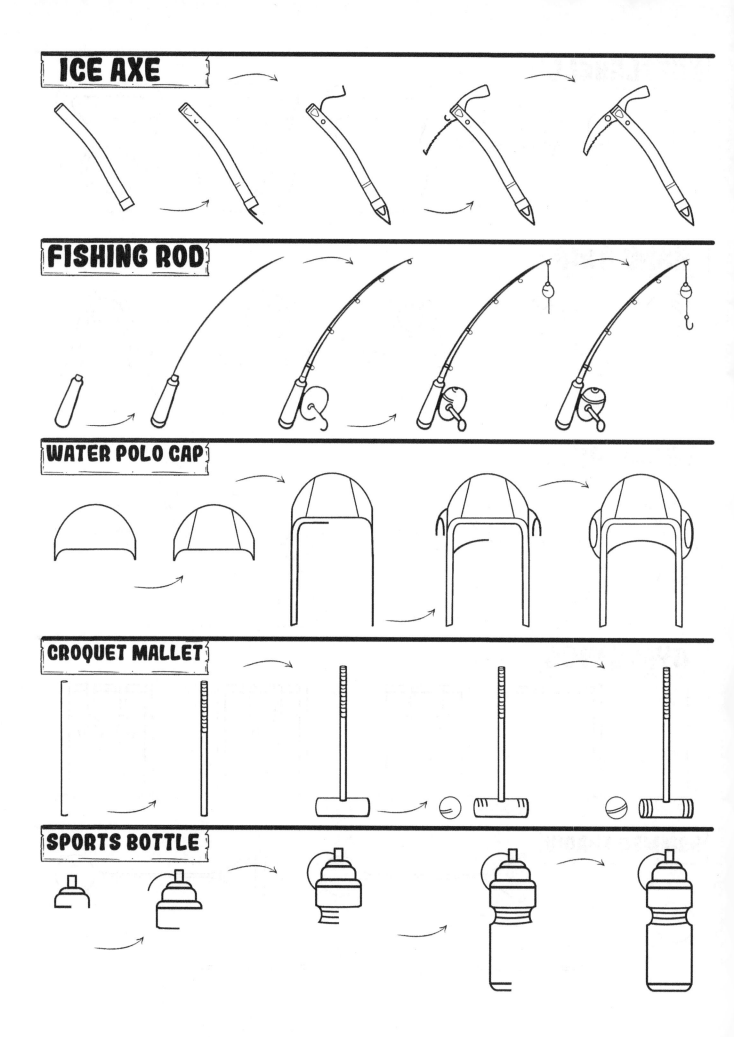

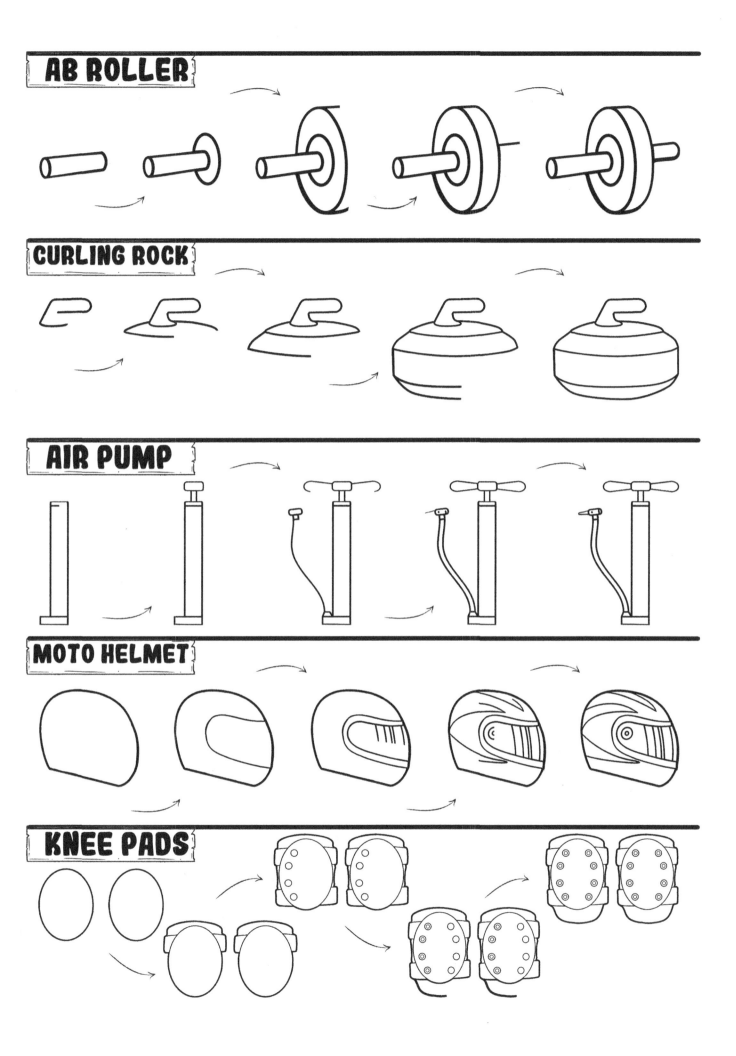

AB ROLLER

CURLING ROCK

AIR PUMP

MOTO HELMET

KNEE PADS

Made in the USA
Las Vegas, NV
28 November 2024